CAMBRIDGE | Discovery
EDUCATION

UNLOCK

READING & WRITING SKILLS 3

Carolyn Westbrook

CAMBRIDGE
UNIVERSITY PRESS

University Printing House, Cambridge CB2 8BS, United Kingdom

Cambridge University Press is part of the University of Cambridge.

It furthers the University's mission by disseminating knowledge in the pursuit of education, learning and research at the highest international levels of excellence.

www.cambridge.org
Information on this title: www.cambridge.org/9781107615267

© Cambridge University Press 2014

First published 2014

Printed in China by Golden Cup Printing Co. Ltd

A catalogue record for this publication is available from the British Library

ISBN 978-1-107-61526-7 Reading and Writing 3 Student's Book with Online Workbook
ISBN 978-1-107-61404-8 Reading and Writing 3 Teacher's Book with DVD
ISBN 978-1-107-61872-8 Listening and Speaking 3 Student's Book with Online Workbook
ISBN 978-1-107-61872-8 Listening and Speaking 3 Teacher's Book with DVD

Additional resources for this publication at www.cambridge.org/unlock

CONTENTS

MAP OF THE BOOK

UNIT	VIDEO	READING	VOCABULARY	
1 ANIMALS Reading 1: Endangered species (zoology) Reading 2: Losing the battle for survival (zoology)	Sharks	*Key reading skill*: Reading for main ideas Using your knowledge to predict content Reading for detail Working out meaning from content Using visuals to predict content Skimming Making inferences from the text	Academic adjectives 1 (e.g. *common, healthy, endangered*)	
2 CUSTOMS AND TRADITIONS Reading 1: Customs around the world (Sociology) Reading 2: A British wedding (Cultural studies)	Customs in Dagestan	*Key reading skill*: Reading for detail Scanning to predict content Reading for main ideas Making inferences from the text Understanding key vocabulary Previewing Skimming Understanding discourse	Academic adjectives 2 (e.g. *brief, certain, obvious*)	
3 HISTORY Reading 1: Museum brochures (History) Reading 2: Should we teach history? (Education)	Egyptian archaeology	*Key reading skill*: Identifying purpose and audience Using your knowledge to predict content Understanding key vocabulary Scanning to find information Skimming Reading for detail Making inferences from the text	Academic vocabulary (e.g. *display, document, period*)	
4 TRANSPORT Reading 1: Masdar: The future of cities? (Transport management) Reading 2: Solving traffic congestion (Urban planning)	Indian transport	*Key reading skill*: Using visuals to predict content Understanding key vocabulary Reading for main ideas Reading for detail Making inferences from the text	Collocation (e.g. *traffic congestion, public transport, rush hour*) Academic synonyms (e.g. *prevent, select, consider*)	
5 ENVIRONMENT Reading 1: Our changing planet (Physical geography) Reading 2: What are the causes of deforestation and what are its effects on the natural environment? (Natural sciences)	Alaskan glaciers	*Key reading skill*: Scanning to find information Using your knowledge to predict content Reading for main ideas Reading for detail Identifying purpose Previewing Understanding key vocabulary Making inferences	Academic vocabulary (e.g. *annual, issue, predict*) Topic vocabulary (e.g. *deforestation, climate change, flood*)	

GRAMMAR	CRITICAL THINKING	WRITING
Comparative adjectives *Grammar for writing*: • Word order, using *and*, *but* and *whereas*	• Analyze a diagram for information • Evaluate information from a diagram	*Academic writing skills*: • Punctuation: capital letters, full stops, commas *Writing task type*: Write two comparison paragraphs. *Writing task*: Compare and contrast the two sharks in the diagram.
Avoiding generalizations with *can* and *tend to* Adverbs of frequency *Grammar for writing*: • Adding detail for interest • Prepositional phrases	• Analyze a description • Identify the structure of a description	*Academic writing skills*: • Essay structure *Writing task type*: Write three descriptive paragraphs. *Writing task*: Describe the laws and traditions concerning weddings. Have there been any changes in recent years?
Making suggestions *Grammar for writing*: • Stating opinions • Linking contrasting sentences with *but, however, although* and *on the other hand*	• Analyze different opinions • Evaluate the importance of information • Organize ideas in a chart	*Academic writing skills*: • Write an introduction *Writing task type*: Write a balanced opinion essay. *Writing task*: Should museums be free or should visitors pay for admission? Discuss.
Grammar for writing: • First conditional • Using *if … not* and *unless*	• Analyze an essay question • Evaluate advantages and disadvantages • Create your own list of advantages and disadvantages	*Academic writing skills*: • Write a conclusion *Writing task type*: Write a problem–solution essay based on a map. *Writing task*: Describe the traffic problems in this city and outline the advantages and disadvantages of the suggested solutions.
Grammar for writing: • Cause and effect • Using *because* and *because of*	• Evaluate ideas and examples using an ideas map • Create your own ideas and examples/evidence	*Academic writing skills*: • Write a topic sentence. *Writing task type*: Write two cause–effect paragraphs. *Writing task*: Outline the human causes of climate change. What effects will these have on the planet?

UNIT	VIDEO	READING	VOCABULARY	
6 HEALTH AND FITNESS Reading 1: Keep fit (Medicine) Reading 2: Tackling obesity (Nutrition)	Cycling	***Key reading skill***: Reading for detail Understanding key vocabulary Using your knowledge to predict content Skimming Reading for main ideas Using key vocabulary Making inferences from the text	Academic verbs and nouns (e.g. *injure, suffer, encourage*) Collocation (e.g. *life expectancy, serious illness, junk food*)	
7 DISCOVERY AND INVENTION Reading 1: The magic of mimicry (Science and technology) Reading 2: The world of tomorrow (Product design)	Robots	***Key reading skill***: Scanning to predict content Using your knowledge to predict content Skimming Reading for detail Making inferences from the text	Understanding prefixes (e.g. *misunderstand, underperform, unsafe*)	
8 FASHION Reading 1: Is fast fashion taking over? (Retail management) Reading 2: Offshore production (Human resources)	Missoni Italian fashion	***Key reading skill***: Distinguishing fact from opinion Using your knowledge to predict content Reading for main ideas Reading for detail Making inferences from the text Understanding key vocabulary Skimming	Hyponyms (e.g. *fashion* and *clothing, beauty products* and *cosmetics*) Homonyms (e.g. *approach, volume, goal*)	
9 ECONOMICS Reading 1: How should you invest your money? (Business) Reading 2: How times have changed (Economics)	The Russian economy	***Key reading skill***: Skimming Understanding key vocabulary Reading for main ideas Identifying purpose Reading for detail Making inferences from the text Using your knowledge to predict content	Academic vocabulary (e.g. *economy, finance, industry*) Synonyms (e.g. *purchase* and *buy, domestic* and *household*)	
10 THE BRAIN Reading 1: Tricks played by the brain (Psychology) Reading 2: Mind control (Neurology)	The amazing brain	***Key reading skill***: Previewing Skimming Reading for detail Making inferences from the text Scanning to predict content	Medical language (e.g. *surgery, vaccination, treatment,*) Academic verbs (e.g. *recover, care, confirm*)	

GRAMMAR	CRITICAL THINKING	WRITING
Grammar for writing: • Giving reasons • Giving examples with *such as, for instance, for example, especially*	• Understand and subdivide arguments • Apply subdivided arguments to the organization of an essay plan	**Academic writing skills**: • Write supporting sentences. **Writing task type**: Write a problem-solution essay. **Writing task**: What can people do to live longer? What can a government do to increase the average life expectancy of its country's citizens?
Making predictions with *will, could* and *won't* **Grammar for writing**: • Relative clauses • Advantages and disadvantages	• Remember ideas clearly by listing advantages and disadvantages • Understand an issue by finding reasons and evidence to support ideas	**Academic writing skills**: • Edit for common errors **Writing task type**: Write an advantage–disadvantage essay. **Writing task**: Choose one new area of technology or invention and outline its advantages and disadvantages.
Grammar for writing: • Prepositional phrases (e.g. *apart from, rather than, along with*) • Counter-arguments (e.g. *argue, claim, insist, state*)	• Evaluate arguments and counter-arguments	**Academic writing skills**: • Cohesion • Coherence **Writing task type**: Write a balanced opinion essay. **Writing task**: Fashion is harmful. Discuss.
Grammar for writing: • Describing graphs – noun phrases and verb phrases • Using prepositions and conjunctions to add data • Writing approximations of numerical data (e.g. *nearly, more than, approximately*)	• Understand and interpret visual information • Analyze a graph	**Academic writing skills**: • Writing a description of a graph **Writing task type**: Write an explanatory paragraph describing a graph **Writing task**: Describe both graphs and explain the data.
Grammar for writing: • Passive (in narrative tenses and with modal verbs)	• Analyze a diagram to understand a process	**Academic writing skills**: • Writing a description of a process **Writing task type**: Write a process paragraph **Writing task**: Explain how the body responds to changes in temperature.

UNLOCK UNIT STRUCTURE

The units in *Unlock Reading & Writing Skills* are carefully scaffolded so that students are taken step-by-step through the writing process.

UNLOCK YOUR KNOWLEDGE	Encourages discussion around the theme of the unit with inspiration from interesting questions and striking visuals.

WATCH AND LISTEN	Features an engaging and motivating *Discovery Education™* video which generates interest in the topic.

READING 1	Practises the reading skills required to understand academic texts as well as the vocabulary needed to comprehend the text itself.

READING 2	Presents a second text which provides a different angle on the topic in a different genre. It is a model text for the writing task.

LANGUAGE DEVELOPMENT	Practises the vocabulary and grammar from the Readings in preparation for the writing task.

CRITICAL THINKING	Contains brainstorming, evaluative and analytical tasks as preparation for the writing task.

GRAMMAR FOR WRITING	Presents and practises grammatical structures and features needed for the writing task.

ACADEMIC WRITING SKILLS	Practises all the writing skills needed for the writing task.

WRITING TASK	Uses the skills and language learnt over the course of the unit to draft and edit the writing task. Requires students to produce a piece of academic writing. Checklists help learners to edit their work.

OBJECTIVES REVIEW	Allows students to assess how well they have mastered the skills covered in the unit.

WORDLIST	Includes the key vocabulary from the unit.

This is the unit's main learning objective. It gives learners the opportunity to use all the language and skills they have learnt in the unit.

UNLOCK MOTIVATION

UNLOCK YOUR KNOWLEDGE

Work with a partner. Discuss the questions below.

1 Is it better to see animals in a zoo or in the wild? Why?
2 Are there more wild animals in your country now or were there more in the past? Why?
3 Why do people keep domestic animals in their homes?
4 What things do we need animals for?
5 Which animals do you think are going to die out in the near future?
6 Can we live without animals?

PERSONALIZE

Unlock encourages students to bring their own knowledge, experiences and opinions to the topics. This motivates students to relate the topics to their own contexts.

DISCOVERY EDUCATION™ VIDEO

Thought-provoking videos from *Discovery Education™* are included in every unit throughout the course to introduce topics, promote discussion and motivate learners. The videos provide a new angle on a wide range of academic subjects.

> The video was excellent! It helped with raising students' interest in the topic. It was well-structured and the language level was appropriate.
>
> Maria Agata Szczerbik,
> United Arab Emirates University,
> Al-Ain, UAE

UNL⌀CK CRITICAL THINKING

> The Critical thinking sections present a difficult area in an engaging and accessible way.
>
> Shirley Norton, London School of English, UK

BLOOM'S TAXONOMY

CREATE — create, invent, plan, compose, construct, design, imagine

decide, rate, choose, recommend, justify, assess, prioritize — EVALUATE

ANALYZE — explain, contrast, examine, identify, investigate, categorize

show, complete, use, classify, examine, illustrate, solve — APPLY

UNDERSTAND — compare, discuss, restate, predict, translate, outline

name, describe, relate, find, list, write, tell — REMEMBER

BLOOM'S TAXONOMY

The Critical Thinking sections in *Unlock* are based on Benjamin Bloom's classification of learning objectives. This ensures learners develop their **lower-** and **higher-order thinking skills**, ranging from demonstrating **knowledge** and **understanding** to in-depth **evaluation**.
The margin headings in the Critical Thinking sections highlight the exercises which develop Bloom's concepts.

LEARN TO THINK

Learners engage in **evaluative** and **analytical tasks** that are designed to ensure they do all of the thinking and information-gathering required for the end-of-unit writing task.

CRITICAL THINKING

Organizing information
Organizing information from a diagram is an important critical thinking skill.

ANALYZE

1 Look at the diagram of the two sharks and the boxes in Exercise 2. Write a sentence for each feature to explain how the sharks are similar or different.

1 Size: _____
2 Colour: _____
3 Skin pattern: _____
4 Mouth: _____
5 Fins and tail: _____

Large tropical sharks

Whale shark

tail

fin

no teeth

Human

UNLOCK RESEARCH

THE CAMBRIDGE LEARNER CORPUS ⊙

The **Cambridge Learner Corpus** is a bank of official Cambridge English exam papers. Our exclusive access means we can use the corpus to carry out unique research and identify the most common errors learners make. That information is used to ensure the *Unlock* syllabus teaches the most **relevant language**.

THE WORDS YOU NEED

Language Development sections provide vocabulary and grammar building tasks that are further practised in the **UNLOCK ONLINE** Workbook. The glossary and end-of-unit wordlists provide definitions, pronunciation and handy summaries of all the key vocabulary.

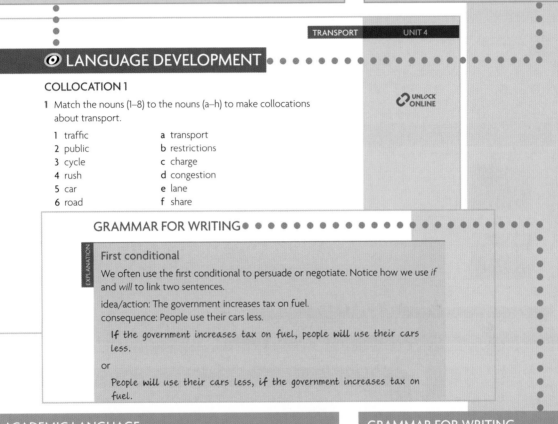

| TRANSPORT | UNIT 4 |

⊙ LANGUAGE DEVELOPMENT

COLLOCATION 1

1 Match the nouns (1–8) to the nouns (a–h) to make collocations about transport.

UNLOCK ONLINE

1	traffic	a	transport
2	public	b	restrictions
3	cycle	c	charge
4	rush	d	congestion
5	car	e	lane
6	road	f	share

GRAMMAR FOR WRITING

EXPLANATION

First conditional

We often use the first conditional to persuade or negotiate. Notice how we use *if* and *will* to link two sentences.

idea/action: The government increases tax on fuel.
consequence: People use their cars less.

> If the government increases tax on fuel, people will use their cars less.

or

> People will use their cars less, if the government increases tax on fuel.

ACADEMIC LANGUAGE

Unique research using the **Cambridge English Corpus** has been carried out into academic language, in order to provide learners with relevant, academic vocabulary from the start (CEFR A1 and above). This addresses a gap in current academic vocabulary mapping and ensures learners are presented with carefully selected words they will find essential during their studies.

GRAMMAR FOR WRITING

The grammar syllabus is carefully designed to help learners become good writers of English. There is a strong focus on sentence structure, word agreement and referencing, which are important for **coherent** and **organized** academic writing.

> " The language development is clear and the strong lexical focus is positive as learners feel they make more progress when they learn more vocabulary.
>
> Colleen Wackrow,
> Princess Nourah Bint Abdulrahman University, Al-Riyadh, Kingdom of Saudi Arabia "

UNL⌀CK SOLUTIONS

FLEXIBLE

Unlock is available in a range of print and digital components, so teachers can mix and match according to their requirements.

UNL⌀CK ONLINE WORKBOOKS

The **UNL⌀CK ONLINE** Workbooks are accessed via activation codes packaged with the Student's Books. These **easy-to-use** workbooks provide interactive exercises, games, tasks, and further practice of the language and skills from the Student's Books in the Cambridge LMS, an engaging and modern learning environment.

CAMBRIDGE LEARNING MANAGEMENT SYSTEM (LMS)

The Cambridge LMS provides teachers with the ability to track learner progress and save valuable time thanks to automated marking functionality. Blogs, forums and other tools are also available to facilitate communication between students and teachers.

UNL⌀CK EBOOKS

The *Unlock* Student's Books and Teacher's Books are also available as interactive eBooks. With answers and *Discovery Education*™ videos embedded, the eBooks provide a great alternative to the printed materials.

COURSE COMPONENTS

- Each level of *Unlock* consists of two Student's Books: **Reading & Writing** and **Listening & Speaking** and an accompanying Teacher's Book for each. Online Workbooks are packaged with each Student's Book.
- Look out for the **UNLOCK ONLINE** symbols in the Student's Books which indicate that additional practice of that skill or language area is available in the Online Workbook.
- Every *Unlock* Student's Book is delivered both in print format and as an interactive **eBook for tablet devices**.
- The *Unlock* Teacher's Books contain additional writing tasks, tests, teaching tips and research projects for students.
- *Presentation Plus* **software for interactive whiteboards** is available for all Student's Books.

READING AND WRITING

Student's Book and Online Workbook Pack*	978-1-107-61399-7	978-1-107-61400-0	978-1-107-61526-7	978-1-107-61525-0
Teacher's Book with DVD*	978-1-107-61401-7	978-1-107-61403-1	978-1-107-61404-8	978-1-107-61409-3
Presentation Plus (interactive whiteboard software)	978-1-107-63800-6	978-1-107-65605-5	978-1-107-67624-4	978-1-107-68245-0

*eBook available from **www.cambridge.org/unlock**

LISTENING AND SPEAKING

Student's Book and Online Workbook Pack*	978-1-107-67810-1	978-1-107-68232-0	978-1-107-68728-8	978-1-107-63461-9
Teacher's Book with DVD*	978-1-107-66211-7	978-1-107-64280-5	978-1-107-68154-5	978-1-107-65052-7
Presentation Plus (interactive whiteboard software)	978-1-107-66424-1	978-1-107-69582-5	978-1-107-63543-2	978-1-107-64381-9

*eBook available from **www.cambridge.org/unlock**

The complete course audio is available from **www.cambridge.org/unlock**

LEARNING OBJECTIVES

Watch and listen	Watch and understand a video about sharks
Reading skills	Identify the main ideas in a text
Academic writing skills	Structure and punctuate a paragraph
Writing task	Write two comparison paragraphs

UNL⟳CK YOUR KNOWLEDGE

Work with a partner. Discuss the questions below.

1 Is it better to see animals in a zoo or in the wild? Why?
2 Are there more wild animals in your country now or were there more in the past? Why?
3 Why do people keep domestic animals in their homes?
4 What things do we need animals for?
5 Which animals do you think are going to die out in the near future?
6 Can we live without animals?

WATCH AND LISTEN

PREPARING TO WATCH

USING YOUR
KNOWLEDGE TO
PREDICT CONTENT

1 You are going to watch a video about sharks. Before you watch, discuss the questions below with a partner.

1 Which shark species is shown in the photograph?
2 What size do these sharks grow to?
3 What kind of prey do sharks eat?
4 Why do sharks attack humans?
5 Do sharks ever attack boats?

2 ▶ Watch the video and check your answers.

3 Complete the short paragraph using the words in the box.

UNDERSTANDING
KEY VOCABULARY

> fatal   prey   mistake   hunters   attack   dangerous

Swimming near sharks can be very (1)_____ because of the risk of an attack. Sharks are very good at locating their food, so they are considered expert (2)_____ . They (3)_____ their (4)_____ at high speed. In other words, they swim to their food very quickly. As a result, they may bite humans by (5)_____ . This can be (6)_____ because the person may drown or lose a lot of blood.

UNLOCK READING AND WRITING SKILLS 3

WHILE WATCHING

4 ▶ Watch again and circle the correct answer (a–c) to complete the statement below.

UNDERSTANDING MAIN IDEAS

The video is about great white sharks and

a the speed they swim in the water.

b how they hunt seals and fish in South Africa.

c why they sometimes attack humans.

5 ▶ Match the sentence halves. Then watch again and check your answers.

UNDERSTANDING DETAIL

1 Great white sharks mainly eat seals and	a 60,000 seals that swim there.
2 Every year, great white sharks kill	
3 Sharks come to False Bay in South Africa for the	b they mistake us for seals.
	c 40 kph, swimming up from deep down in the bay.
4 Great white sharks kill seals by crashing into them at	d large sea creatures like tuna.
5 Great white sharks will attack a carpet in the shape of a seal because	e if they look like a fish.
6 Even though they are meat-eaters, sharks will bite into plants	f an average of three people.
7 Sharks prefer fish to humans but attack humans because	g they cannot tell the difference at high speeds.

6 Work with a partner. Try to answer the questions below.

MAKING INFERENCES

1 Why did the shark bite into the boat in the video?

2 Why do the seals risk swimming in the water with sharks?

3 Why do sharks prefer seals and tuna to humans?

DISCUSSION

7 Work with a partner. Discuss the questions below.

1 Should we be worried about sharks when we swim in the sea?

2 Should we protect sharks from fishing?

3 What are the benefits of research into animal behaviour?

READING 1

PREPARING TO READ

USING YOUR
KNOWLEDGE TO
PREDICT CONTENT

1 Complete the table below with the names of any endangered animals and extinct animals you know.

endangered animals	extinct animals

2 Scan the factsheet on page 19 opposite and add any animals mentioned to your list of endangered animals.

WHILE READING

READING FOR
MAIN IDEAS

UNLOCK
ONLINE

3 Read the factsheet and match the main ideas (1–4) to the paragraphs where they are mentioned (A–D).

1 How hunting and overfishing cause animals to become endangered _____
2 The difference between endangered and extinct animals _____
3 How governments and normal people can protect animals _____
4 How humans destroy and pollute animal habitat _____

Reading for the main ideas

Read the first sentence or two of each paragraph to understand the main idea.

READING
FOR DETAIL

4 Look at the bold words in the questions below. Which paragraph (A–D) of the factsheet should you look at to find each answer?

1 Who are most responsible for animal **extinctions** and **endangered** species? _____
2 Why does **pollution** and **chopping down trees** cause problems for animals? _____
3 What do people **hunt animals** for? _____
4 Which **large sea creatures** have become endangered because of overfishing? _____
5 What can **individuals** do to protect animal species from becoming endangered? _____
6 What should **governments** do about hunting and fishing of animals? _____
7 What should **governments** invest in to get more animals back into the wild? _____

Endangered species

A An endangered species is a group of animals that could soon become extinct. Extinction happens when the last of the species has died out and there will be no more. Many species are nearly extinct and could disappear off the face of the earth very soon if we don't do anything to save them. There are many reasons why species become endangered but most of them are due to humans. However, there are things that we can do to save endangered species.

B Habitat destruction is the main reason why animals become endangered and this happens in two ways. When humans move into a new area, the animals' habitat – where they live – is destroyed and there is nothing to eat because humans chop down trees and build houses and farms. Animal habitats are also destroyed because of pollution. Chemicals in rivers and poisons on farms cause the destruction of habitats and animals can no longer live there.

C Endangered species are also the result of hunting and fishing. Animals such as the Arabian oryx have been hunted to the edge of extinction because of the high price of their meat. Other animals are killed for their fur, bones or skin, or just for sport. Some seal species are now on the verge of extinction because they are killed for their fur to make coats. Tigers are shot to make medicine and tea from their bones, and crocodiles are caught to make bags and shoes. Overfishing means that large sea creatures like whales, tuna and sharks have all become endangered species, because too many are caught to make things like shark's fin soup.

D So what can individuals and governments do to protect animal and plant species from becoming endangered? We should take care not to pollute natural areas, and farmers or companies who destroy animal habitats should face a financial penalty. The public can help out by refusing to buy any products that are made from animals' body parts, such as seal fur coats or crocodile bags. Governments can help, too, by making it against the law to hunt, fish or trade in endangered species. They can also provide funding for animal sanctuaries and zoos, to protect animals from extinction by breeding more endangered animals, which they later release into the wild. If we all cooperate by taking these steps, we will protect our planet so that our children and their children can enjoy it too.

5 Read the factsheet again and answer the questions (1–7) in Exercise 4.

READING BETWEEN THE LINES

6 Read the last paragraph of the factsheet and underline words and phrases that mean the same as the bold words below.

1 Companies who destroy animal habitats should **pay a fine**.
2 Individuals should help to protect animals by **choosing not to buy** products like fur.
3 The government can make it **illegal** to hunt, fish or trade in endangered species.
4 Governments can **pay for** animal sanctuaries and zoos.
5 If we **work together** by **taking this action**, we can protect our planet.

DISCUSSION

7 Work with a partner. Discuss the questions below.

1 What other endangered species do you know about?
2 Should the government spend money to save animal habitats even if this means less money for roads or hospitals?

READING 2

PREPARING TO READ

1 Work with a partner. Look at the photographs and discuss the questions below.

1 What are the animals in the photographs?
2 Do you have them in your country?
3 Which animal is more successful in Britain?
   Why do you think this is?

WHILE READING

2 Skim the article below and find three reasons why the red squirrel is losing the battle for survival.

3 Read the article and answer the questions.

1 How many red squirrels are left in the UK?
2 Which squirrel is larger?
3 What are the four reasons given for the success of the grey squirrel in the UK?

UNLOCK
ONLINE

Losing the battle for survival

Red squirrels used to be a common sight in British forests and countryside. However, fewer than 140,000 individuals are thought to be left and most of them are found in Scotland. In contrast, grey squirrels are now so common they are seen as a pest and can be legally trapped and destroyed. The population decrease in red squirrels is claimed to be due to the introduction of the grey squirrel from North America, but disease and the loss of its native woodland habitat have also played a major role in the decline of the red squirrel in Britain.

On first sight, the two species of squirrel are similar. They both have a distinctive long tail, which helps the squirrel to balance when jumping from tree to tree, and the same large eyes, small ears and powerful back legs. However, the grey squirrel has a clear physical advantage over the red. The red squirrel has a typical head-and-body length of 19 to 23 centimetres, a tail length of 15 to 20 centimetres and a body weight of 250 to 340 grams. Compared to this, the grey squirrel is a larger animal. The head and body measures between 23 and 30 centimetres long and the tail is between 19 and 25 centimetres long. Adult grey squirrels are heavier, weighing between 400 and 600 grams. This size allows them to store more fat and helps them to survive a harsh winter, which would be fatal to their smaller cousins.

So why are red squirrels losing out in competition with grey squirrels? Size is one factor but there are others. Red squirrels live high up in trees, whereas greys spend more of their time on the ground. This means that any reduction in forest habitat greatly affects the red squirrel population. Another reason for the grey squirrel's success is its ability to use food provided by humans. Like the fox, the grey squirrel can survive in an urban environment because of its intelligence and adaptability. The other problem for the red squirrel is disease. Both squirrels carry the parapox virus. While this does not seem to affect grey squirrels, it is fatal to reds.

There does not seem to be much we can do to help red squirrels survive. Some politicians support destroying populations of grey squirrels but this would be seen as cruel by most people in Britain. However, red squirrels have been successfully introduced from other countries and they could be effectively protected in places like the Isle of Wight and Anglesey, where there are no grey squirrels. Another question is whether we should protect red squirrels at all. Worldwide, they are not an endangered species, so many scientists would prefer government conservation funding to be spent on other endangered animals.

4 Read the summary below and circle the correct words to complete it.

The article compares the red and the grey squirrel. The [1]*grey / red* squirrel was introduced to Britain and has become very successful since then. Now there are [2]*fewer / more* than 140,000 native red squirrels left in the wild, but the grey is regarded as a [3]*pest / pet*. The main reason why the red squirrel is less successful is that the grey squirrel is [4]*fatter / thinner* so it is less affected by cold weather. Another reason is that grey squirrels are [5]*unable / able* to live in cities. A further reason may be the parapox virus, which [6]*kills / injures* red squirrels. [7]*Most / Few* British people support destroying grey squirrels and because red squirrels [8]*are / aren't* endangered worldwide, they could be reintroduced to the UK.

READING BETWEEN THE LINES

5 Look again at the article on page 21 and try to answer the questions below.

1 Why do you think grey squirrels are regarded as a pest?
2 Who do you think are the 'smaller cousins' mentioned in paragraph two?
3 Why might some British politicians be in favour of saving the red squirrel?
4 Why do you think there are no grey squirrels on Anglesey and the Isle of Wight?

DISCUSSION

6 Work with a partner. Discuss the questions below.

1 Should we save British red squirrels
   a by killing grey squirrels?
   b by planting more trees?
   c by trying to protect them from disease?
2 Is trying to save British red squirrels a waste of time and money?
3 Are introduced animal species a problem in your country?

⊙ LANGUAGE DEVELOPMENT

ACADEMIC ADJECTIVES 1

UNLOCK ONLINE

1 Match the adjectives (1–7) to their definitions (a–g).

1 endangered	a	unkind and unpleasant
2 aggressive	b	strong and well
3 healthy	c	easy to recognize
4 cruel	d	facing a high risk of extinction
5 familiar	e	seen in a lot of places
6 common	f	not strong
7 weak	g	behaving in an angry or violent way

Comparative adjectives

When we compare things, we have to use the comparative form of the adjective.

2 Complete the table below using the adjectives in the box. The first one in each category has been done for you as an example.

> common   healthy   endangered   small
> aggressive   weak   familiar   heavy

one-syllable adjective	two- (or more) syllable adjective	two-syllable adjective ending with -y
adjective + **-er** + **than**	*more/less* + adjective + *than*	adjective + **-ier** + **than**
1 weaker than 2 _____	3 more familiar than 4 _____ 5 _____ 6 _____	7 heavier than 8 _____

3 Use comparative forms from the table to complete the sentences below.

1 The red squirrel is smaller and _____ the grey squirrel.

2 Grey squirrels are generally _____ their smaller cousins, because greys are not affected by the parapox virus.

3 Great white sharks are _____ tiger sharks, which are not at risk of extinction.

4 Whale sharks are _____ tiger sharks and do not attack anything.

CRITICAL THINKING

At the end of this unit, you will write two comparison paragraphs. Look at this unit's Writing task in the box below.

> Compare and contrast the two sharks in the diagram.

Organizing information

Organizing information from a diagram is an important critical thinking skill.

ANALYZE

1 Look at the diagram of the two sharks and the boxes in Exercise 2. Write a sentence for each feature to explain how the sharks are similar or different.

1 Size: _____

2 Colour: _____

3 Skin pattern: _____

4 Mouth: _____

5 Fins and tail: _____

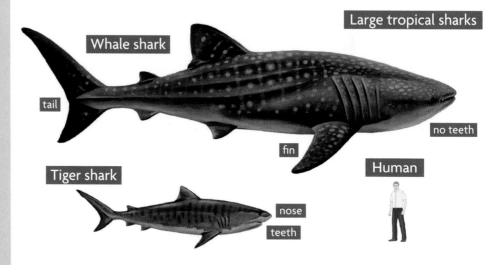

EVALUATE

2 Look at more information about the two sharks and answer the questions on page 25 opposite.

Whale shark	**Tiger shark**
Length – 10 metres	Length – 4 metres
Weight – 9 tonnes	Weight – 500 kg
Diet – plankton, krill, other very small animals	Diet – tuna, dolphins, turtles
Conservation status – endangered	Conservation status – not currently at risk of extinction
Behaviour towards humans – no recorded attacks	Behaviour towards humans – 119 attacks since 2009

1 Which shark is smaller?
2 Which shark is heavier?
3 Which shark uses its teeth to eat large prey?
4 Which shark filters tiny sea creatures from water?
5 Which shark is less endangered?
6 Which shark is more dangerous?
7 Why do you think one of the sharks attacks humans and the other one does not?

WRITING

GRAMMAR FOR WRITING

EXPLANATION

Word order

In English, the subject (S) usually comes before the verb (V) and the object (O). These example sentences show other common features of English word order.

S	V	O
Squirrels	eat	seeds, nuts and fruit.

S	V	adjective	prepositional phrase
Grey squirrels	are	common	in Britain.

linker	S	V	prepositional phrase
However,	they	were introduced	from North America.

1 Use some of the words in the box above to label the different parts of grammar in the sentences below.

1 The tiger shark doesn't hunt in fresh water.

2 However, the whale shark isn't aggressive.

3 The tiger shark has markings on its skin.

4 The whale shark has a large mouth and eats plankton.

Using *and, or, but* and *whereas*

Using words to join sentences together can make our text flow better.

When we join the two sentences together, we can also take out some words so we don't repeat them. This makes the sentences shorter and better, because we can avoid repetition and fit more information into our writing.

2 Look at sentences (a–e) below. Answer the questions.

   1 What is the difference between the first three lines (a–c) below?

   2 What is the difference between the use of *and* and *or* in the sentences (a–e)?

   a **The tiger shark has** sharp teeth. **The tiger shark has** a powerful bite.

   b **The tiger shark has** sharp teeth **and the tiger shark has** a powerful bite.

   c **The tiger shark has** sharp teeth **and** a powerful bite.

   d **The whale shark does not have** sharp teeth. **The whale shark does not have** a powerful bite.

   e **The whale shark does not have** sharp teeth **or** a powerful bite.

3 Join the pairs of sentences below with *and* or *or*. Take out the repeated words.

   1 The **whale** shark is light blue. The **whale** shark has dots on its body.

   _____

   2 The **tiger** shark is dark blue. The **tiger** shark has a stripe pattern on its body.

   _____

   3 The **tiger** shark eats large sea creatures. The **tiger** shark is dangerous to humans.

   _____

   4 The **whale** shark is not aggressive. The **whale** shark is not dangerous to swim with.

   _____

   5 The **tiger** shark is not an endangered species. The **tiger** shark is not a protected species.

   _____

   6 The **whale** shark is an endangered species. The **whale** shark is protected from fishing.

   _____

4 Look at the example below, which shows how to contrast two sentences using *whereas*. Then link the pairs of sentences above (1–2, 3–4 and 5–6) in the same way, using *but* or *whereas*.

> The tiger shark has sharp teeth **and** a powerful bite, **whereas** the whale shark does not have sharp teeth **or** a powerful bite.

EXPLANATION

Using *both* and *neither*

We can use other phrases to compare two different things. If two things/people have the same characteristic, we can use *both ... and ...* .

Both the grey squirrel **and** the red carry the parapox virus.

If they do not have a particular characteristic, we can use *neither ... nor ...* .

Neither the grey squirrel **nor** the red are found in the north of Scotland.

5 Write sentences using the information in the table below.

	red squirrels	grey squirrels
1 have long tails	Yes	Yes
2 live on the Isle of Man	No	No
3 are meat-eaters	No	No
4 are an endangered species	No	No
5 live in forests	Yes	Yes

ACADEMIC WRITING SKILLS

Punctuation

When we write, we need to use correct punctuation. We always start a new sentence with a *capital letter* and usually end it with a *full stop*. We use capital letters for names of countries, cities and people. We use *commas* when we write a list of adjectives or nouns. We also use a comma before *whereas* and after *however*.

1 Correct the punctuation of the sentences (1–5) below.

1 however the whale shark has to be protected in countries in asia like taiwan and the philippines because it is so slow and easy to catch

2 the whale shark is a large slow-moving fish with wide fins a long tail and a huge mouth

3 this gentle giant is not dangerous to humans and divers can swim with it touch it and even ride on its back fin

4 it does this by ram feeding which means it swims fast to force water and animals into its mouth

5 it uses this mouth to eat very small plants and animals like krill plankton and algae

Paragraph structure

We start a paragraph with a topic sentence, which introduces or defines the topic. We follow this with supporting sentences, which give extra information about the topic. We end the paragraph with a concluding sentence, which sums up the paragraph and links back to the topic sentence.

2 Put the sentences in Exercise 1 in order to make a paragraph that starts with a topic sentence, has supporting sentences in the middle and ends with a concluding sentence.

WRITING TASK

UNLOCK
ONLINE

> Compare and contrast the two sharks in the diagram.

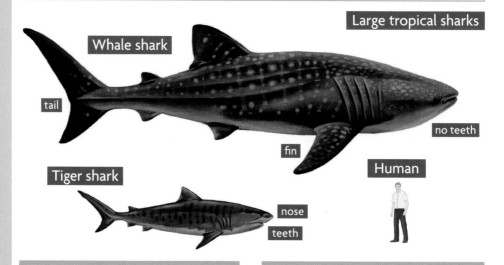

Large tropical sharks

Whale shark

tail

no teeth

fin

Tiger shark

Human

nose

teeth

Whale shark

Length – 10 metres
Weight – 9 tonnes
Diet – plankton, krill, other very small animals
Conservation status – endangered
Behaviour towards humans – no recorded attacks

Tiger shark

Length – 4 metres
Weight – 500 kg
Diet – tuna, dolphins, turtles
Conservation status – not currently at risk of extinction
Behaviour towards humans – 119 attacks since 2009

1 Read the introduction and the conclusion of the essay below, which compares and contrasts the two sharks. Then complete the essay by comparing three or four features of the sharks in each of the two supporting paragraphs.

> The diagram gives information about two kinds of large tropical shark, the whale shark and the tiger shark.
>
> The sharks have a number of differences in terms of size, shape and colour.

_____
_____
_____
_____
_____
_____
_____
_____

> The sharks are also different in terms of diet, behaviour and conservation status.

_____
_____
_____
_____
_____
_____
_____

> Overall, it is clear that the whale shark is a much larger animal, but it is a gentle giant, whereas the smaller tiger shark is much more dangerous.

2 Use the checklist to review your paragraphs for content and structure.

TASK CHECKLIST	✔
Have you used a topic sentence to introduce each paragraph?	
Have you included measurements from the diagram to add detail?	
Have you compared three or four features and included what is similar, as well as what is different, about the sharks?	

3 Make any necessary changes to your paragraphs.

4 Now use the language checklist to edit your paragraphs for language errors which are common to B1 learners.

LANGUAGE CHECKLIST	✔
Have you used comparative adjectives correctly?	
Have you used *and, or, but, whereas, neither* and *both* correctly?	
Have you used capital letters, commas and full stops correctly?	

5 Make any necessary changes to your paragraphs.

OBJECTIVES REVIEW

6 Check your objectives.

I can ...

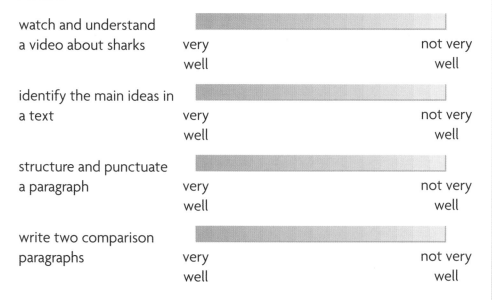

watch and understand
a video about sharks

very
well

not very
well

identify the main ideas in
a text

very
well

not very
well

structure and punctuate
a paragraph

very
well

not very
well

write two comparison
paragraphs

very
well

not very
well

WORDLIST

UNIT VOCABULARY	ACADEMIC VOCABULARY
attack (n)	aggressive (adj)
extinction (n)	common (adj)
fatal (adj)	cruel (adj)
habitat (n)	endangered (adj)
hunt (v)	familiar (adj)
hunting (n)	weak (adj)
overfishing (n)	

LEARNING OBJECTIVES

Watch and listen	Watch and understand a video about customs in Dagestan
Reading skills	Read for detail
Academic writing skills	Structure an essay
Writing task	Write three descriptive paragraphs

UNL⌀CK YOUR KNOWLEDGE

Work with a partner. Discuss the questions below.

1 Which celebration is shown in the photograph?
2 What customs and traditions do visitors to your country need to know?
3 What traditional celebrations do you have in your country?

WATCH AND LISTEN

PREPARING TO WATCH

USING VISUALS TO
PREDICT CONTENT

1 Work with a partner. Look at the photographs and try to answer the
questions below.

   1 Where do you think the photographs were taken?

   2 Is it a rural area or an urban area?

   3 Is it a traditional region or a modern region?

   4 What industry do you think is in the area?

   5 Do you think people live in nuclear families that include just the
     parents and children, or extended families that include children, parents
     and grandparents?

2 ▶ Watch the video and check your answers. Now choose the best
description of the topic of the video.

   a Industry   **b** Weddings   **c** Culture   **d** Family life

WHILE WATCHING

UNDERSTANDING
MAIN IDEAS

3 ▶ Watch the video and number the ideas (a–h) in the order that you
hear them. Not all the ideas are mentioned.

   a holidays   _____

   b languages   _____

   c history   _____

   d family networks   _____

   e traditional industry _____

   f marriage   _____

   g migration   _____

   h law   _____

4 ▶ Watch again and correct the factual mistakes in the sentences below.

1 Dagestan is smaller than Scotland.

2 Dagestan is in Russia.

3 Thirty-five languages are spoken in the region.

4 Carpet-making is done by machine.

5 Younger people are local leaders.

6 The population of Dagestan is declining.

7 Dagestanis want to be buried in the capital city.

5 Which words and phrases (a–i) are mentioned in relation to carpet-making in Dagestan?

a traditional

b modern designs

c local

d cotton

e wool

f thread

g vegetables

h galleries

i museums

6 Work with a partner. Answer the questions below.

1 Why are Dagestani carpets so popular?

2 Why do many Dagestanis live outside the country?

DISCUSSION

7 Work with a partner. Discuss the questions below about your country.

1 What are some traditional industries?

2 Do young people stay in the country or do they move away? Why do they make this choice?

3 Discuss family life.

a What is family life like there?

b Are extended families or nuclear families more popular?

c What do young people like to do?

PREPARING TO READ

1 Scan the magazine article opposite for the words and phrases in the box and underline them each time they appear.

> kiss   shake hands   touch   gift   dress

2 Answer the questions below, according to the information in the article. Use the text around the words you have underlined to help you.

1 In which countries should you not kiss your business partner?

_____

2 In which countries do men shake hands when they meet each other?

_____

3 In which country do people touch each other when they are talking?

_____

4 In which country is it common to give a present at a business meeting?

_____

5 In which country is it unlucky to give white flowers?

_____

WHILE READING

3 Read the article on page 37 opposite. Which of the customs (a–g) below are not mentioned?

a greetings
b personal space
c giving gifts
d business meetings
e table manners
f giving business cards
g being punctual

CUSTOMS
AROUND THE WORLD

As more and more people travel all over the world, it is important to know what to expect in different countries and how to react to cultural differences so that you don't upset your foreign contacts. In our 'Customs around the world' series, we look at three different cultures every month to help you prepare for that important trip. This month's locations are Brazil, Japan and India.

BRAZIL

Brazilians are very friendly people and are generally informal, so it is important to say hello and goodbye to everyone. Women kiss men and each other on the cheek but men usually just shake hands. Brazilians stand very close to each other and touch each other's arms, elbows and back regularly while speaking. You should not move away if this happens. If you go to a business meeting, you are not expected to take a gift. In fact, an expensive gift can be seen as suspicious.

On the other hand, if you're invited to someone's house, you should take a gift – for example, flowers or chocolates. However, stay clear of anything purple or black, as these colours are related to death.

If you are invited to dinner, arrive at least 30 minutes late, but always dress well because appearances are very important to Brazilians.

JAPAN

The Japanese are quite different from the Brazilians. They can be quite formal, so don't stand too close. Kissing or touching other people in public is not common. When you meet someone, they may shake your hand, although bowing is the more traditional greeting.

In a business meeting, Japanese people often like to know what your position is in your company before they talk to you. You should hand over a business card using both hands and when you receive a business card, you should immediately read it carefully. It is important to be punctual in Japan. It is recommended that you arrive early and dress formally. Gifts are often exchanged, but it is common to refuse before you accept them. When you present your gift, you should say that it is just a token of your appreciation.

Most visitors are entertained in a restaurant, so it is a great honour to be invited to a Japanese person's house.

INDIA

Hierarchy is important in India, so when you meet Indians, it is important to greet the oldest or the most senior person first. Men may shake hands with men, and women often also shake hands with women, but men and women tend not to shake hands. When leaving, you should say goodbye to everyone individually.

Personal relationships are important in business in India and you should not be surprised if the first meeting is spent getting to know everyone. In addition, it is important to know that many Indians do not like to say 'no', so it may be difficult to know what they are really thinking. Appointments are necessary and punctuality is important. Business dress is formal, so men and women should wear dark suits.

If you are invited to an Indian's home, arrive on time. You do not have to bring a gift but gifts are not refused. However, do not bring white flowers, because these are used in funerals.

4 Match the sentence halves. Then read the article again and check your answers.

1 In Brazil, women kiss men and each other on the cheek, but men
2 Taking a gift to a business meeting
3 If you are going to a Brazilian's house for dinner, you
4 Bowing is a common way to
5 In Japan it is very impolite to
6 Spend time getting to know everyone when you
7 In India and Japan punctuality is very important, so you should

a is not a good idea in Brazil.
b arrive on time.
c put away a business card without studying it first.
d do not kiss each other.
e meet Indian business partners.
f greet Japanese people.
g can arrive late.

Reading for detail

Reading for detail is an important part of academic reading and it is a skill which is tested in many language examinations. Look for key words in the text and pay attention to words like *not*, *however* and *but* which show contrasting views or information.

READING BETWEEN THE LINES

5 Work with a partner. Try to answer the questions below.

1 In Brazil, why would people be suspicious of an expensive gift?
2 Why shouldn't you move away if Brazilians touch you during conversation?
3 Why is it important for Japanese business people to know your position in a company?
4 Why do Indians not like to say 'no'?
5 Why is it important to know about other people's customs?

DISCUSSION

6 Work with a partner. Discuss the questions below.

1 Have you ever been abroad? Where?
2 Which country would you like to visit? Why?
3 What advice about customs in your country would you give a visitor?

READING 2

PREPARING TO READ

UNDERSTANDING KEY VOCABULARY

1 Match the words and phrases (1–9) to their definitions (a–i).

1 legal requirement
2 registry office
3 engagement ring
4 groom
5 marriage certificate
6 wedding ceremony
7 bride
8 wedding list
9 reception

a the event during which the couple are married
b the man who is going to get married
c the woman who is going to get married
d in Britain, a non-religious building where you can get married
e a document which shows all the different presents that a couple would like to receive for their wedding
f something that you need to do according to the law
g a celebration or meal which takes place after the wedding ceremony
h a ring which is given as a promise to marry
i a piece of paper which proves that two people are married

PREVIEWING

2 Work with a partner. Look at the title on page 40 and try to answer the questions below.

1 How old are most people when they get married in Britain?
2 On average, how many guests are invited to British weddings?
3 Are British attitudes to marriage changing or staying the same?

3 Now read the page from a citizenship guide on page 40 and check your answers.

WHILE READING

SKIMMING

4 Choose the best summary.

a The text describes traditional British weddings and says how the traditions are changing.
b The text contrasts traditional and modern relationships in Britain.
c The text describes marriage customs around the world and in the UK.
d The text describes what happens on a traditional wedding day in Britain.

UNLOCK ONLINE

A BRITISH WEDDING

Weddings are important occasions in British life. They can be very expensive and take a long time to organize. There are also many traditional aspects of weddings that are important for people who get married. However, many traditions have become less common in recent years and marriage in Britain is changing.

Marriage is legal from the age of 18, but this can be lowered to 16 if the couple have their parents' permission. The average age of people who get married in the UK is about 30. People can marry in a civil ceremony, at a registry office, or they may have a religious ceremony in a church, mosque or other place of worship. All couples must sign a marriage certificate. This is a legal document which proves that they are married. Divorced men and women can remarry but this may not be possible in a church.

In the past, a traditional marriage in the UK meant a couple first got engaged. This was when the man formally asked the woman to marry him with a ring. It was also traditional, for the groom to ask the bride's father if he agreed. The wedding commonly took place at the bride's local church with about a hundred guests. It was a tradition for the groom's father to buy the flowers and champagne but for the bride's father to pay for everything else. The two families sat on different sides of the church and the bride's father gave away his daughter to the groom. Female friends and family members helped her with her long dress and were called bridesmaids. The couple exchanged rings, kissed and then signed the marriage certificate. When they left the church, guests threw paper confetti at them and took a lot of photographs. Everyone then went to a hotel or restaurant for the wedding reception and they had a meal, made speeches and danced. The guests brought wedding presents for the couple's new home and the couple then went on a long holiday called a honeymoon. The new bride took her husband's surname.

These days, however, many people do not always follow tradition so closely. It is now common for the woman to ask the man to marry her, and not many men ask the woman's father for her hand in marriage. People frequently marry in a town hall. A few even marry on a beach in a hot country. The couple tend to pay for the wedding themselves but still expect both families to help them pay for the reception. These days not every woman wants to change her surname so she might keep her maiden name or take both names.

5 Correct the factual mistakes in the sentences below.

1 Weddings in the UK are cheap and easy to organize.

2 Most people get married between the ages of 35 and 40.

3 Couples can choose to sign a marriage certificate if they want to.

4 Divorced men and women can remarry in a church.

5 When a couple get engaged, the woman gives the man a ring.

6 The bride's father gives his daughter away and helps her with her dress.

7 After the wedding ceremony, the guests take wedding presents to the couple's new home.

8 Nowadays, the groom's father pays for the reception and the couple pay for the rest.

READING BETWEEN THE LINES

6 Scan the guide and circle the word *this* each time you see it. What does *this* refer to in the following phrases?

1 this can be lowered to 16
2 this is a legal document
3 this may not be possible in a church
4 this is when the man asks the woman to marry him

DISCUSSION

7 Work with a partner. Discuss the questions below.

1 What happens in a traditional wedding ceremony in your country?
2 Are any of the traditional celebrations in your country changing? How?

◉ LANGUAGE DEVELOPMENT

Avoiding generalizations

In academic English, we have to be careful not to make general statements unless we have the data to prove them. A reader of the example sentence below can argue that not all weddings are expensive.

> Weddings are expensive.

Notice how we avoid generalizations by using *can* or *tend to*.

Modal verb

> Weddings **can** <u>be</u> expensive.

Verb

> Weddings **tend to** <u>be</u> expensive.

Notice the second verb (*be*) is in the infinitive form.

UNL◑CK ONLINE

1 Use the words in brackets to avoid generalizations in sentences (1–5).

   1 We tip the waiter in restaurants. (tend to)

   _____

   2 Weddings are less common these days. (tend to)

   _____

   3 Birthdays are important. (can)

   _____

   4 Blowing your nose in public is rude in Japan. (can)

   _____

   5 Shaking hands is how most people greet you in India. (tend to)

   _____

Adverbs of frequency

We can also use adverbs of frequency to avoid generalizations. Notice the position of the adverbs in the sentences below.

Before the main verb

> People **usually** have barbeques in summer.
> Weddings can **sometimes** take place in hotels.

After the verb *to be*

> Weddings are **often** difficult to organize.

2 Use the words in brackets to avoid generalizations in sentences (1–5).

1 The bride's family pays for the wedding. (usually)

_____

2 People go for picnics in the countryside at weekends. (often)

_____

3 Professionals can get upset if you don't use their correct title. (sometimes)

_____

4 Cultural knowledge is important in business situations. (frequently)

_____

5 It is best to arrive on time for an appointment. (usually)

_____

ACADEMIC ADJECTIVES 2

3 Replace the words in bold in the sentences (1–7) below with the academic adjectives in the box.

> brief   certain   obvious   common
> important   serious   separate

1 The wedding service was very **short** and we went straight to the reception. _____

2 Divorce is a **bad** problem in this country. _____

3 The bride and groom live in **different** houses until after the wedding. _____

4 In **some** countries, marriage is becoming less popular. _____

5 People wanted to marry into **powerful** families for money and status. _____

6 Some customs and traditions are not **clear** for people new to the country. _____

7 It is not **usual** for people in my country to have large families. _____

CRITICAL THINKING

At the end of this unit, you will write three descriptive paragraphs. Look at this unit's Writing task in the box below.

> Describe the laws and traditions concerning weddings in your country. Have there been any changes in recent years?

ANALYZE

1 In order to analyze a description, we need to identify the parts and its structure. Look back at Reading 2 on page 40 and complete the table with information about traditional British weddings.

Law	UK	Your country
age	marriage is legal at (1)_____ most people marry at (2)_____	
documents	both people sign a (3)_____	
place	people marry at a (4)_____	

Proposal		
people	the man may ask the woman's (5)_____	
gift	the man gives a (6)_____	

Wedding day		
people	(7)_____ guests	
cost	(8)_____ pays for the wedding (9)_____ pays for the flowers	
name	the bride usually takes (10)_____	
reception	– at a (11)_____ or restaurant – have (12)_____ – make (13)_____ dance – afterwards, go on a (14)_____	

2 Look back at the last paragraph of Reading 2. Which items in the table on page 44 opposite have changed recently?

APPLY

3 Look at the table again. Complete the third column with information about the customs and traditions of weddings in your country or region. You may need to add new categories to the chart.

4 Use a different colour to circle on the table where any of the customs and traditions have changed in recent years.

WRITING

GRAMMAR FOR WRITING

Adding detail for interest

To make our writing more interesting we can add more detail.

1 Look at the simple sentence below. Match the more detailed sentences (1–5) to the methods used for adding detail (a–e).

> Weddings are important.

1 Weddings are very important.
2 Traditional weddings are very important.
3 Traditional weddings are very important to many people.
4 In my country, traditional weddings are very important to many people.
5 In my country, traditional weddings tend to be very important to many people.

a add words to avoid generalizations
b add a prepositional phrase
c add two prepositional phrases
d add an adjective to a noun
e add an adverb to an adjective

2 For each sentence (1–3), add the words and phrases in the box to make a longer, more detailed sentence. More than one answer is possible.

1 There is a wedding reception.

> large   with hundreds of guests
> after the ceremony   often

2 The man gives a ring.

> to show they are engaged   diamond
> expensive   may   to his fiancée

3 The guests bring wedding gifts.

> at the reception   wrapped   usually
> for the bride and groom

ACADEMIC WRITING SKILLS

Essay structure

An essay should have an introduction which shows the organization of the essay. It should have an appropriate number of main body paragraphs with topic sentences which link back to the topics in the introduction. It should also have a conclusion which summarizes the topics in the paragraphs and links back to the introduction.

1 Look at the essay question and the introduction of an essay written in response to it. This introduction shows the paragraph order of the essay by listing the topics of each paragraph. What are the three topics the writer intends to describe in the essay?

Describe the laws and traditions concerning weddings in your country. Have there been any changes in recent years?

Weddings are very important occasions in my country. They are vital social events which join two families together to celebrate the new marriage. In this essay, I will describe the law concerning marriage where I live, outline the customs and traditions of a typical wedding and show how weddings have changed in recent years.

2 This introduction shows there are three paragraphs in the main body of the essay. Look back at the Critical thinking section on page 44 and plan the supporting sentences for each paragraph.

Paragraph 2 – Law
age –
people –
documents –
place –

Paragraph 3 – Typical wedding
proposal –
people –
location –
cost –
events –

Paragraph 4 – Changes
age –
cost –
proposal –
name –

WRITING TASK

UNLOCK ONLINE

WRITE A
FIRST DRAFT

EDIT

> Describe the laws and traditions concerning weddings in your country. Have there been any changes in recent years?

1 Use the introduction provided on p46 and the supporting sentences in your plan to write an essay to answer the question in the writing task.

2 Use the task checklist to review your essay for content and structure.

TASK CHECKLIST	✔
Have you got an introduction and three main paragraphs on different parts of the topic?	
Have you given all the important information about the wedding?	
Have you answered the second question, not just the first one?	

3 Make any necessary changes to your essay.

4 Now use the language checklist to edit your essay for language errors which are common to B1 learners.

LANGUAGE CHECKLIST	✔
Have you replaced general adjectives with academic words?	
Have you used the language to avoid generalizations?	
Have you included extra adjectives, nouns and prepositional phrases to make sentences longer and more detailed?	

5 Make any necessary changes to your essay.

OBJECTIVES REVIEW

6 Check your objectives.

I can ...

watch and understand a video about customs in Dagestan

very well · not very well

read for detail

very well · not very well

structure an essay

very well · not very well

write three descriptive paragraphs

very well · not very well

WORDLIST

UNIT VOCABULARY	ACADEMIC VOCABULARY
bride (n)	brief (adj)
engagement ring (n)	certain (adj)
fiancé (n)	common (adj)
fiancée (n)	important (adj)
groom (n)	obvious (adj)
legal requirement (n)	separate (adj)
marriage certificate (n)	serious (adj)
punctual (adj)	
reception (n)	
registry office (n)	
tend (v)	
wedding ceremony (n)	
wedding list (n)	

LEARNING OBJECTIVES

Watch and listen	Watch and understand a video about archaeology
Reading skills	Identify purpose and audience of a text
Academic writing skills	Write an introduction
Writing task	Write a balanced opinion essay

UNLOCK YOUR KNOWLEDGE

Work with a partner. Discuss the questions below.

1 Does your country have a long history?

2 What are the most important periods and events in your country's history?

3 Why are some people uninterested in history?

WATCH AND LISTEN

PREPARING TO WATCH

USING VISUALS TO PREDICT CONTENT

1 You are going to watch a video about archaeology. Look at the photographs above and answer the questions below.

1 Where were the photographs taken?
2 What are the people doing in the photographs?
3 Why are people interested in this subject?

UNDERSTANDING KEY VOCABULARY

2 Complete the sentences below using the words in the box.

> archaeologist   hieroglyphics   excavation
> tomb   artefact   remains

1 The ancient Egyptian system of writing is called _____ .
2 An _____ is someone who studies the objects of people who lived in the past.
3 Someone's dead body or the remaining parts of it are called their _____ .
4 A _____ is a large stone structure or underground room where someone is buried.
5 An _____ is removal of the earth which is covering very old objects, to discover things about the past.
6 An _____ is an ancient object in a museum.

WHILE WATCHING

3 ▶ Watch the video and number the main ideas (a–g) in the order that you hear them.

a the archaeological season _____

b examining and recording _____

c ancient Egyptian kings _____

d modern X-ray equipment _____

e excavation on the site _____

f the Valley of the Kings _____

4 ▶ Match the sentence halves. Then watch again and check your answers.

1 It is illegal to

2 Hidden underground, these painted tombs and fragile artefacts

3 Before any discoveries can be made

4 It is a time-consuming task but

5 Every new find must be carefully recorded and

6 Every year, archaeologists continue to

a the site is so delicate, heavy machinery is not allowed.

b look for more evidence of this advanced culture.

c excavate or remove artefacts without permission.

d there is alway a large amount of earth and sand to move first.

e have been preserved by the dry air of the desert.

f nothing can be moved until it is photographed.

5 Work with a partner. Try to answer the questions below.

1 Why do you think the archaeological season starts in October?

2 Why are only a few archaeologists allowed to excavate artefacts?

3 Why do you think security is tight at the archaeological sites?

4 Why do the artefacts need to be recorded, photographed and preserved before they are moved from the archaeological site?

DISCUSSION

6 Work with a partner. Discuss the questions below.

1 Are there any important historical sites in your country? If so, which ones?

2 Why are these sites important for us today?

READING 1

PREPARING TO READ

USING YOUR
KNOWLEDGE TO
PREDICT CONTENT

1 Work with a partner. Discuss the questions below.

1 What kinds of museums are there in your country?
2 Should schools take children to museums as part of their education? Why / Why not?
3 How can museums make their exhibitions fun for visitors?

UNDERSTANDING
KEY VOCABULARY

2 Match the words and phrases in the box to their definitions (1–9).

> ancient   archaeology   fossil   exhibition   exhibit
> field   knight   natural history   sword

1 the remains of an extinct prehistoric animal or plant
2 the study of human cultural objects and sites from the past
3 an object in a museum
4 the study of plants and animals
5 a display of objects or artworks in a museum or gallery
6 very old
7 area of study
8 a fighting man from the mediaeval period
9 a long weapon that cuts

WHILE READING

SCANNING TO FIND
INFORMATION

UNLOCK
ONLINE

3 You are going to read four brochures about museums. Scan each text and match it to one of the museums (1–4).

1 Warwick Castle   Text _____
2 the Porsche Museum   Text _____
3 the Museum of Science and Industry Chicago   Text _____
4 the Natural History Museum   Text _____

4 Why did each museum produce these brochures?

5 Read the texts on page 55 opposite and answer this question:

SKIMMING

Which museum (A–D) would you visit to do the following?

1 learn ancient fighting techniques
2 look at classic automobiles
3 participate in science experiments
4 discover extinct animal life
5 listen to a guide on headphones
6 produce chemical reactions
7 stay overnight

A

DINO SCENE
INVESTIGATION

Look at rocks and bones, dig up your own fossils, and find out how to identify prehistoric animals and plants at the Natural History Museum. Dinosaurs became extinct around 65 million years ago, so how do we know what they looked like and how they behaved? Bring your pupils to our Dino Scene Investigation workshops to find out!

If you want more from your dinosaur experience, you can actually spend the night in the museum. Our Dino Snores programme takes you into the museum and on your way to your 'bedroom' you solve a puzzle. You can then watch a film before going to sleep under the Diplodocus dinosaur. Although museum admission is free there is a charge for the Dino Snores events, so see the website for details.

B

TEAM-BUILDING
THE MEDIAEVAL WAY

Bring your staff to our special Mediaeval Knight School for a company event they won't forget! Our experienced knights will tell you about the history of Warwick Castle and will take you back to mediaeval times when the Castle's soldiers were getting ready to fight. Your employees will improve their business skills, such as leadership and trust, while they learn about fighting with swords and bows and arrows.

For more information, contact our Sales Team.

C

EXCELLENT
TECHNOLOGICAL
ACHIEVEMENTS
IN MOTORING!

Porsche has a unique history in motor racing and engineering innovation. The Porsche Museum in Stuttgart, Germany has around 80 of the most famous Porsche models in the history of the company. Children can take part in the 'Museum Rallye', which is a quiz relating to the exhibits. There is also a special children's audio guide, which is available in several languages. They can learn about the exhibits in any order and at their own speed. It serves to present the excitement and variety of the Porsche brand to children from all over the world.

D

'LIVE SCIENCE'
EXPERIENCES
AND LEARNING LABS

Our vision is to inspire children to achieve their full potential in the fields of science, technology, engineering and medicine. In our 'Live Science' experiences, you can be an atom and discover which other atoms you bond with, or experiment with gravity by throwing things over the balcony!

In our 'Moving with Newton' Learning Lab, you can learn about Newton's three laws of motion, or take part in our 'Colourful Chemistry' Learning Lab and see what happens when you mix and heat chemicals to produce light and colours.

You'll find this and so much more at the Museum of Science and Industry Chicago!

6 Re-read the texts and choose one activity in each case which is not available.

1 the Natural History Museum
   a digging up fossils
   b recognizing different dinosaurs
   c sleeping inside a dinosaur

2 Warwick Castle
   a handling ancient weapons
   b learning how to be a better leader
   c reading the history of Warwick Castle

3 the Porsche Museum
   a taking part in a model car race
   b listening to a recorded guide
   c participating in a quiz

4 the Museum of Science and Industry Chicago
   a dropping exhibits to demonstrate gravity
   b learning about atomic energy
   c doing basic chemical experiments

READING BETWEEN THE LINES

7 Work with a partner. Discuss statements (1–4) below and circle the best answer (a–c) to complete each one.

1 Sleepovers are offered at the Natural History Museum
   a to attract children to the museum.
   b to sell more museum tickets to adults.
   c to allow more time to visit the museum.

2 Companies use the Mediaeval Knight School at Warwick Castle
   a to learn about sales techniques.
   b to teach staff to fight.
   c to help team-building.

3 Porsche wants to attract children to the museum
   a to inspire children to become engineers in the future.
   b to help advertise the cars.
   c to sell model cars in the gift shop.

4 The goal of the Museum of Science and Industry Chicago is
   a to educate children about chemistry.
   b to make science funny for children.
   c to motivate children to have a career in science.

Identifying purpose and audience

It is useful to think about what the author was trying to do when they wrote the text. This will give us a clue about the organization of the text and its function.

DISCUSSION

8 Work with a partner. Discuss the questions below.

  1 Have you ever visited any museums like these? If so, what are your strongest memories?
  2 Is it better to learn about history from books and the internet or from museums?

READING 2

PREPARING TO READ

1 Match the words and phrases in the box to their definitions (1–7).

> compulsory   ongoing discussion   economic benefits
> less obvious   tuition   knowledgeable   beyond

  1 teaching
  2 unfinished argument
  3 not optional
  4 not very clear
  5 financial advantages
  6 knowing a lot about something
  7 going a long way past something

WHILE READING

UNLOCK ONLINE

2 In the essay on page 58, the writer responds to a question about whether we should teach History. The word *should* appears seven times in the main body of the essay. Do tasks 1–3 below.

  1 Scan the essay and underline the word *should* each time you see it. The first one has been done for you as an example.
  2 Does the writer think we should or should not teach History?
  3 Read the essay in full to check your answer to Question 2 above.

3 Which paragraphs (A–D) mention the points (1–4) below?

  1 reasons why we should teach History   _____
  2 the writer's own opinion   _____
  3 why we should not teach History   _____
  4 the introduction and essay structure   _____

Should we teach History?

A History is still a compulsory subject at lower levels and pupils still choose to study it at higher levels. However, there is an ongoing discussion about whether schools <u>should</u> continue to teach History or whether they should spend the money on other subjects. This essay will deal with the arguments against and in favour of teaching History in school, concluding that we should teach History, because the value of the subject goes beyond the classroom.

B First of all, many pupils suggest that History is one of the less interesting school subjects and that governments should spend the time and money on subjects that are more useful. Some people argue that Maths and English are more important so we can have a society with a good basic education. Other people say that we should spend the money on teaching Science, as this can move a country forward and benefit the economy. However, when we teach History, we are just looking back at the past. The economic benefits of this area are less obvious.

C On the other hand, there are a number of reasons why it is a good idea to teach History. Teaching History is important because students should be able to understand the background to current issues in the news. This will create better-informed citizens. Another reason why teaching History is a good idea is that it helps pupils to understand their culture and background, which also helps them to understand the society they live in. In addition to learning about the past, History tuition can help students to think for themselves. Finally, it also improves pupils' reading and writing skills, which can help them become better students.

D In conclusion, although there are clearly arguments on both sides, it seems to me that we should teach children about the past because the advantages of teaching the subject go beyond the content of the classes. I would say that the teaching of History helps to create generations of well-educated and knowledgeable individuals.

4 Read the essay again and complete the chart using the phrases in the box.

> This knowledge creates better citizens.
> Science benefits the economy.
> Pupils learn about culture.
> Pupils improve reading and writing skills.
> We should focus on Maths and English.

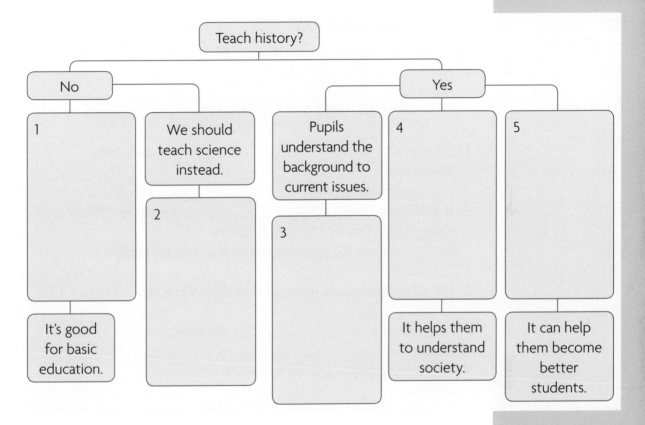

5 Why does the writer include more reasons in favour of teaching History than reasons against?

READING BETWEEN THE LINES

6 Would the writer agree or disagree with these claims? Underline the section of the text which supports your answer.

   1 Government spending on History education should be reduced.

   2 The benefits of History education are useful in further study.

   3 Teaching History brings many economic benefits to a country.

   4 History tuition is just as important as teaching science.

   5 Covering History in the classroom is perhaps a waste of time.

DISCUSSION

7 Work with a partner. Discuss the questions below.

1 Which school subjects are popular with students in your country? Why?
2 Should students and their parents be allowed to choose which subjects they study at school?

⊙ LANGUAGE DEVELOPMENT

ACADEMIC VOCABULARY

1 Complete each pair of sentences using the words in the box. The same word completes each pair.

> display   document   financial   research   period

1 We intend to do new _____ into the site's early development.
The museum has its own _____ programme.
2 The museum needs _____ assistance because it does not make enough money from ticket sales.
Until we applied for government funding, we had terrible _____ problems.
3 The collection houses many ancient texts and a very important legal _____ .
We make sure to _____ each artefact that is found on the site.
4 This room is devoted to life in the late mediaeval _____ in London.
We spent a long _____ of time studying history at school.
5 Museums must ensure that they _____ artefacts with the correct lighting.
The digital _____ at the museum is designed to guide you through the collection.

Making suggestions

When we write an academic essay, we use *should* to make suggestions. However, we may need to make more than one suggestion, so we often use other ways to say *should*.

Look at the sentences below, which show different ways to introduce the topic of your suggestion and highlight it for the reader.

> We should **teach History in schools**.
> It is important to **teach History in schools**.
> **Teaching History in schools** is a good idea.

Notice how we add *-ing* to *teach* when we use it as a noun. This is a good way to make an action (a verb) the subject of your sentence.

2 Look at the statements (1–3) and complete the sentences.

1 We should **pay to visit museums**.
   a It is important to _____ .
   b _____ is a good idea.

2 We should **protect ancient objects from theft**.
   c It is important to _____ .
   d _____ is a good idea.

3 We should **learn from past mistakes**.
   e It is important to _____ .
   f _____ is a good idea.

3 Complete sentences (1–6) using the phrases in the box.

> we should   it is important   is a good idea

1 There are a number of reasons why _____ to teach History.

2 Another reason why teaching History _____ is that it helps with writing skills.

3 It seems to me that _____ pay to visit museums in the same way that we pay for other kinds of entertainment.

4 _____ for children of all ages to be taken to museums.

5 I am not entirely convinced that _____ be charged admission to museums.

6 Some people doubt whether _____ for children to visit museums during school time.

CRITICAL THINKING

At the end of this unit, you will write a balanced opinion essay. Look at this unit's Writing task in the box below.

> Should museums be free or should visitors pay for admission? Discuss.

Organizing ideas

Before we write an essay, we have to organize our ideas so that they flow logically. All ideas that relate to the same point should be grouped together.

ANALYZE

1 Read the opinions of the people (1–4). Who thinks that museums should be free and who thinks people should pay to visit museums?

> **1** The government has far more important things to think about. It needs to fund the emergency services and healthcare rather than invest in the arts.

> **2** There should be no fee to enter a museum. All children, rich or poor, should be able to visit them and smell and touch the artefacts. It makes history so much more interesting than reading about it in a book.

> **3** Museums are very expensive to build and maintain. It seems to me that the public should help pay for the staff, security and building costs.

> **4** I think the government should pay for museums. The history of our country should be preserved for future generations. The state should keep its treasures safe from theft and maintained in good condition.

EVALUATE

2 Complete the chart below using the opinions in Exercise 1 to make a plan for your essay. The first one has been done for you as an example.

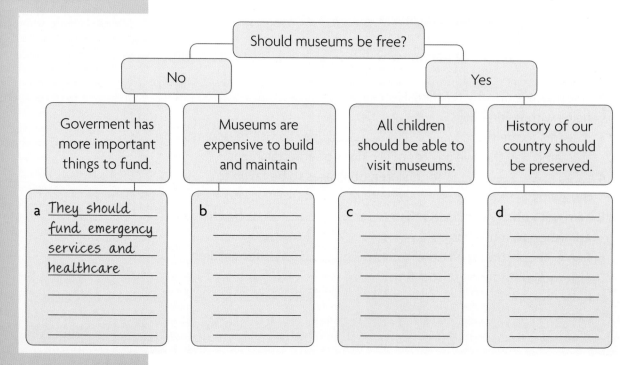

Should museums be free?

No

Goverment has more important things to fund.

a _They should fund emergency services and healthcare_

Museums are expensive to build and maintain

b _____

Yes

All children should be able to visit museums.

c _____

History of our country should be preserved.

d _____

WRITING

GRAMMAR FOR WRITING

EXPLANATION

Stating opinions

When we write an essay, we have to state other people's opinions as well as our own. If we always write *some people think ...*, our essays can sound repetitive, so we try to use a variety of phrases to say the same thing.

Notice how writers use other phrases to avoid repeating *think* when they give their own opinion.

| I think
It seems to me that
I believe that
I would say that | we should teach history. |

Notice how writers use a number of different words to mean *think* when they give the other side of the argument.

| Many people | think
argue
state
claim
suggest
feel | that protecting ancient objects from theft is a good idea. |

UNLOCK ONLINE

1 Rewrite the sentences below using phrases from the explanation box above. The first one has been done for you as an example.

1 History should be replaced by other subjects.
   <u>Many people think that History should be replaced by other subjects.</u>

2 A number of people think that museums should make people pay for entry.

_____

3 I think it would be better to teach foreign languages instead of History.

_____

4 Some people think that students should be made to learn History.

_____

5 I think we need to make museums more interesting for young people.

_____

Linking contrasting sentences

We use *but, however, although* and *on the other hand* before a new idea that is opposed to, or in contrast to, the first idea.

2 Look at the statements (1–5). How is the punctuation different for each statement?

1 Many people feel that museums should charge visitors an entry fee but others claim that museums should be free to all.

2 Many people feel that museums should charge visitors an entry fee, although others claim that museums should be free to all.

3 Many people feel that museums should charge visitors an entry fee. However, others claim that museums should be free to all.

4 Many people feel that museums should charge visitors an entry fee. On the other hand, others claim that museums should be free to all.

5 Although many people feel that museums should charge visitors an entry fee, others claim that museums should be free to all.

3 Rewrite the sentences below using *although*. The first one has been done for you as an example. More than one answer is possible.

1 Museums are free **but** they cost a lot of money to maintain.
Although museums are free, they cost a lot of money to maintain.

2 Museums are free, to allow all children to visit them. However, many children never go to a museum.

_____

3 It is a good idea for governments to pay for museums, but there are many other more important things that a government should spend its money on.

_____

4 Some museums may be quite boring for children. However, nowadays many of them are very interactive.

_____

5 Museums are great places for schools to visit but sometimes they are very expensive.

_____

ACADEMIC WRITING SKILLS

Writing an introduction

The introduction to an essay should lead the reader in to the main body of the essay and give background information which the reader needs in order to understand the topic. It also states the structure of the essay and includes the thesis statement – a sentence which explains the writer's opinion and conclusions from the essay.

1 Look at the different parts of introductions to essays. Match each piece of background information (a–c) to a structuring sentence (1–3) and a thesis statement (i–iii) to make three essay introductions.

Background information		
a Some people think it is important that museums are free, to provide education for children. However, others argue that museums are entertainment, so visitors should be charged to view the collection.	**b** Children sometimes complain that museums are dry and boring places. In order to modernize their image, there is a range of things museums can do to make their exhibitions more fun.	**c** State-funded museums drain the government of money which should be spent on other things, like pensions, healthcare and the police.
Structuring sentence		
1 This essay will suggest that people should pay to enter a museum.	**2** This essay will present the arguments in favour of and against charging for museums.	**3** This essay will suggest solutions for making museums more attractive for children.
Thesis statement		
i I will argue that museums should be free because of their educational value for children.	**ii** I will conclude by explaining why it is important for museums to modernize their collections.	**iii** I will end by explaining how the money spent on museums could be better spent on other things.

2 Which introduction follows the instructions in the writing task and discusses both sides of the argument?

WRITING TASK

WRITE A FIRST DRAFT

> Should museums be free or should visitors pay for admission? Discuss.

1 Using your plan from the Critical thinking section on page 63, complete the essay.

   1 Add the introduction from Exercise 2 in the Academic writing skills section.

   2 Write one paragraph about why museums should not be free.

   3 Write one paragraph about why museums should be free.

   4 Write a concluding paragraph.

2 Use the task checklist to review your essay for content and structure.

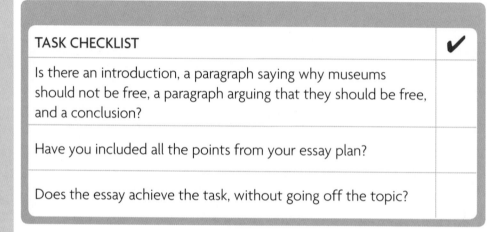

TASK CHECKLIST	✔
Is there an introduction, a paragraph saying why museums should not be free, a paragraph arguing that they should be free, and a conclusion?	
Have you included all the points from your essay plan?	
Does the essay achieve the task, without going off the topic?	

3 Make any necessary changes to your essay.

EDIT

4 Now use the language checklist to edit your essay for language errors which are common to B1 learners.

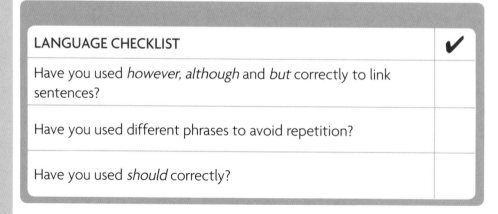

LANGUAGE CHECKLIST	✔
Have you used *however, although* and *but* correctly to link sentences?	
Have you used different phrases to avoid repetition?	
Have you used *should* correctly?	

5 Make any necessary changes to your essay.

OBJECTIVES REVIEW

6 Check your objectives.

I can ...

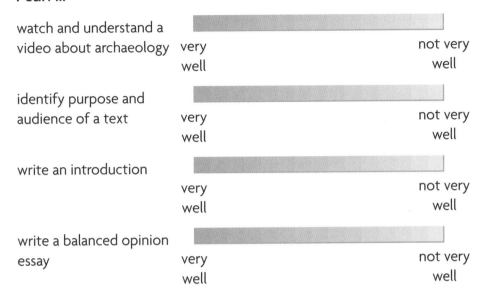

watch and understand a
video about archaeology   very   not very
                            well   well

identify purpose and
audience of a text   very   not very
                            well   well

write an introduction
                            very   not very
                            well   well

write a balanced opinion
essay   very   not very
                            well   well

WORDLIST

UNIT VOCABULARY	ACADEMIC VOCABULARY
ancient (adj)	compulsory (adj)
archaeologist (n)	display (v)
archaeology (n)	document (n)
artefact (n)	economic (adj)
excavation (n)	exhibition (n)
exhibit (n)	field (n)
fossil (n)	financial (adj)
hieroglyphics (n)	period (n)
knight (n)	research (v)
natural history (n)	tuition (n)
sword (n)	

LEARNING OBJECTIVES

Watch and listen	Watch and understand a video about Indian transport
Reading skills	Predict answers from visual clues
Academic writing skills	Write a conclusion
Writing task	Write a problem–solution essay

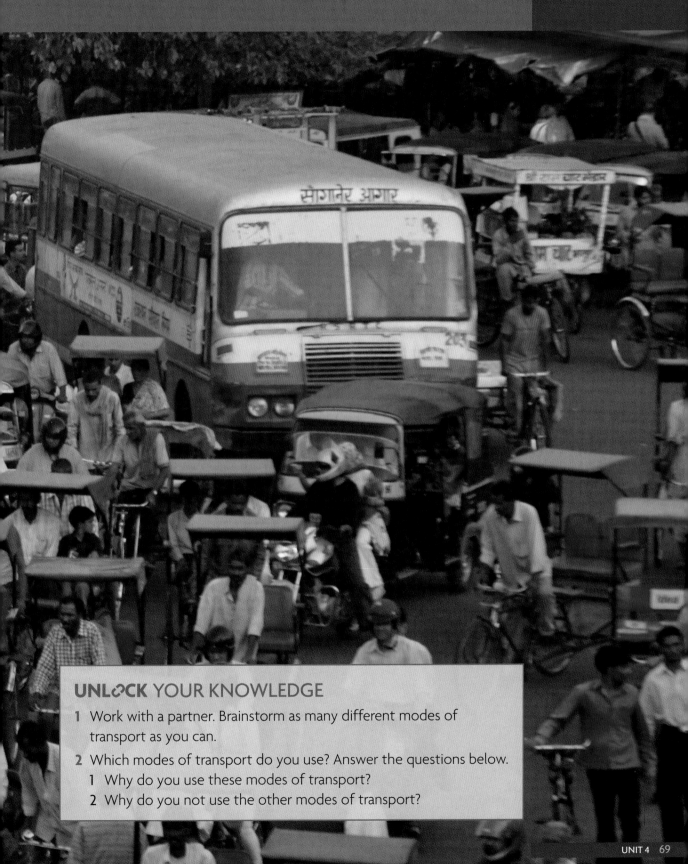

TRANSPORT UNIT 4

PREPARING TO WATCH

USING YOUR KNOWLEDGE TO PREDICT CONTENT

1 You are going to watch a video about transport in India. Before you watch, choose the correct answers (a–d) to the questions (1–6).

1 How many people live in India?
  a 13 million   **b** 0.2 billion   **c** 1.2 billion   **d** 2.2 billion

2 How many cars are there in India?
  a 1.2 million   **b** 13 million   **c** 30 million   **d** 13 billion

3 In 2005, how many households owned a bicycle?
  a 40%   **b** 14%   **c** 30%   **d** 13%

4 When were the railways introduced to India?
  a 1853   **b** 1940   **c** 1947   **d** 1951

5 How many people do Indian railways carry every day?
  a 2.8 million   **b** 13 million   **c** 14 million   **d** 30 million

6 How many staff work for the Indian railways?
  a 7,500   **b** 65,000   **c** 1.4 million   **d** 2.8 million

2 ▶ Watch the video and check your answers.

WHILE WATCHING

LISTENING FOR KEY INFORMATION

3 ▶ Watch the video and complete the notes on page 71 opposite about the different modes of transport using the words in the box.

> father   rural   centuries   passengers   freight   ban
> transport   afford   systems   stations   efficient

Water taxis

Used for (1)_____
Take thousands of (2)_____ along the river
every day
Boats are handed from (3)_____ to son

Ox carts

Traditional in (4)_____ India
Some cities (5)_____ ox carts because of traffic
problems

Bicycles

A common mode of (6)_____ in India
Now more people can (7)_____ to own a bicycle

Trains

In 1947, there were 42 railway (8)_____
7,500 (9)_____
2.8 million tonnes of (10)_____ daily
Railways are very (11)_____

4 Complete the table below with one advantage and one disadvantage of each mode of transport shown in the video.

UNDERSTANDING DETAIL

mode of transport	advantages	disadvantages
1 water taxis	_____	_____
2 ox carts	_____	_____
3 bicycles	_____	_____
4 trains	_____	_____

DISCUSSION

5 Work with a partner. Discuss the questions below.

1 What is the public transport like in your country?
2 Do you use public transport at home and abroad? Why? / Why not?

READING 1

PREPARING TO READ

USING VISUALS TO PREDICT CONTENT

1 Work with a partner. Look at the photographs of transport in two cities and try to answer the questions below.

1 What problem can you see in the first photograph?
2 How could the vehicle in the second photograph be a solution to this problem?
3 What do you think is different about the city in the second photograph?

UNDERSTANDING KEY VOCABULARY

2 Match the words and phrases in the box to their definitions (1–9) below.

> commuting time   rapid transit   traffic congestion   vehicle
> major issue   outskirts   vandalism   route   carbon-neutral

1 the areas that form the edge of a town or city
2 a way or road between places
3 how long it takes to get to work from home
4 too many cars and lorries close together and unable to move
5 big problem
6 the crime of damaging property
7 not releasing any CO_2 into the atmosphere, or compensating for CO_2 release through a reduction by investing in renewable energy
8 a machine used for transport
9 fast transport

WHILE READING

READING FOR MAIN IDEAS

3 Read the case study on page 73 opposite and answer the questions (1–5).

1 What is a PRT?
2 In addition to the PRT, how will Masdar City be better designed than older cities?
3 Apart from the PRT, what other transport options are available in Masdar City?
4 What is the main problem with Masdar City's planned PRT system?
5 How does the PRT work?

The expanding economy and rising population have brought great benefits to Abu Dhabi but with them comes a major issue: traffic jams. Abu Dhabi, like many UAE cities, has a major issue with traffic congestion, and, although it is not as bad as in some cities, the average commuting time of 45 minutes is quite high.

Abu Dhabi's answer to this is Masdar City, a new city being built near the airport on the outskirts of Abu Dhabi. Masdar, which means 'source', is a city which gets all of its electricity from the environment by using renewable energy sources such as solar power. There is a wall around the city to keep out the hot desert wind and the streets are narrow. There is therefore more shade from the sun, and the breeze passes through the streets better. As a result, the city is about 15 °C cooler than Abu Dhabi.

There is no traffic congestion in the six-kilometre-square city of Masdar because cars are not allowed in the city. Instead, people use public transport. There is an underground rail system and a Light Rail Transit system, which run through the centre of the town and connect Masdar to Abu Dhabi and the airport. A Personal Rapid Transit system (PRT) was also planned. This is a system of small, personalised, electric machines that run on solar energy. They are controlled wirelessly and move by being pulled along by magnets along their route. The plan was that 3,000 'podcars', which can carry 2 to 6 passengers, would drive people to about 100 stations all around the city and also take them from outside the city, where they would leave their cars, to their destination in the city.

The problem is that the costs of building Masdar City are substantial: it was projected to cost around US $24 billion, but the global financial crisis of 2008–9 had a negative effect on the plans. Planners now have to find a way to build the PRT at a much lower cost. The dream of a carbon-neutral, congestion-free city could become reality in the future but there are other issues. There is the risk of vandalism for the PRT and also safety concerns about these pilotless cars. However, if all of the problems are solved, the benefits of Masdar City's green solutions to both traffic and environmental problems will certainly outweigh the financial investment in the longer term.

Masdar
the future of cities?

4 Complete the sentences below using no more than three words.

1 Abu Dhabi has a big problem with _____ .
2 The average time it takes to get to work is _____ .
3 Masdar's electricity comes from _____ .
4 Traffic jams are not a problem in Masdar because cars are _____ in the city.
5 Instead, people travel around using _____ .
6 In 2008–09 Masdar suffered the negative effects of the _____ .

READING BETWEEN THE LINES

5 Work with a partner. Try to answer the questions below.

1 How did the 2008–9 global financial crisis affect the Masdar City project?
2 Why could the PRT be a target for vandalism?
3 What are the safety concerns for a PRT system?

DISCUSSION

6 Work with a partner. Discuss the questions below.

1 Would you like to live in Masdar City? Why / Why not?
2 Do you agree that the benefits of Masdar City will outweigh the financial cost?
3 Would a PRT system work in your city? Why / Why not?

READING 2

PREPARING TO READ

Using visuals to predict content

The images which accompany a text can provide valuable information on the content.

1 Work with a partner. You are going to read an essay about solving traffic congestion. Look at the photographs on page 75 opposite and try to answer the questions below.

1 What solutions to the problem of traffic congestion do the photographs show?
2 What other solutions to traffic congestion can you think of?
3 Read the essay and check your answers.

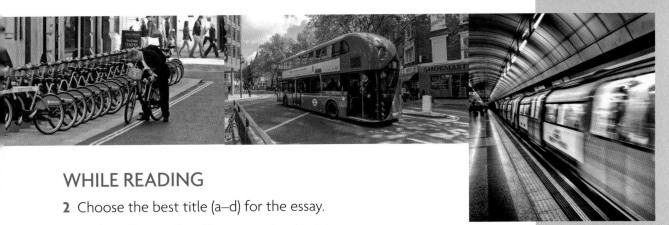

WHILE READING

2 Choose the best title (a–d) for the essay.

a The effects of traffic congestion in cities

b Solving traffic congestion

c Urban traffic congestion is increasing

d Bicycles can solve urban traffic congestion

Many of the world's big cities have problems with congestion. There is simply far too much traffic, so governments everywhere have to think about how to solve the problem.

Traffic jams have a number of negative effects. They cause stress to drivers, which may lead to health problems or road rage. They can also reduce productivity because products cannot be delivered on time and employees arrive late for work or meetings. Another important issue is that the emergency services can become caught in traffic. Finally, there are the negative effects that traffic congestion causes to the environment. Traffic congestion wastes fuel, which in turn produces more carbon dioxide through the car exhausts and contributes to the greenhouse effect.

However, there are a number of steps that can be taken to reduce road congestion. The most obvious solutions involve engineering. This means building more roads with wider lanes so that more cars can travel at the same time. Tunnels and bridges can be constructed in order to reduce the congestion that happens when cars have to stop at traffic lights. However, the problems with these kind of solutions are the construction costs and that more roads may actually encourage more traffic.

Other, more creative solutions to the congestion problem are to increase tax on fuel so that it is more expensive, or make people pay to travel on certain roads such as in the centre of a city or on a motorway. If we do this, people are more likely to think carefully about using their car. However, taxing fuel and roads may mean that some people cannot afford to drive their cars and may have to give up their jobs. Also, governments may not want to increase fuel taxation too much if it is unpopular with voters.

A more popular solution, therefore, would be to encourage other forms of transport which will lead to fewer cars on the road. One suggestion is to encourage people to cycle more. Although this mode of transport has obvious health benefits and reduces air pollution, it is not very practical in every climate and can prove dangerous in heavy traffic.

Another possibility is to persuade people to use buses. This means many people can travel in just one vehicle. However, generally, people dislike the image travelling by bus creates. A park and ride system can allow people to drive to the edge of cities, park and then take a bus to the city centre. This allows some flexibility for car drivers but reduces city centre congestion. However, the buses tend not to run at night.

Overall, although there are a number of good ways to tackle this problem, some of these also have negative effects. It would seem that encouraging alternative forms of transport is probably the best solution as this solves the congestion problems and reduces the amount of traffic at the same time, which will also have a positive effect on the environment.

3 What are the four effects of traffic congestion mentioned in the essay?

4 Complete the table using one word for each answer.

	solutions	advantages	disadvantages
engineering	Build more roads, (1)_____ and bridges.	More vehicles can (2)_____ at once.	This may (3)_____ more traffic.
tax	Increase tax on roads and (4)_____ .	People will think more about using their cars.	People may need to give up their (5)_____ .
cycling	It will result in fewer cars on the road.	It has benefits for your (6)_____ and reduces pollution.	It can be dangerous when (7)_____ is heavy.
park and ride	People drive to the edge of a city, park their cars and then travel into the city centre by (8)_____ .	It reduces (9)_____ in the city centre.	Buses may not operate at (10)_____ .

READING BETWEEN THE LINES

MAKING
INFERENCES
FROM THE TEXT

5 Work with a partner. Try to answer the questions below.

1 What sort of health problems do you think the author means are caused by stress?
2 Why would a government not want to have an unpopular tax?
3 What is the image problem with using a bus that the author mentions?

DISCUSSION

6 Work with a partner. Discuss the questions below.

1 What is the traffic situation like in your town or city?
2 What has your government done to help with traffic problems?
3 Which of the suggestions above would you recommend and why?
4 Do you have any better suggestions?

⊙ LANGUAGE DEVELOPMENT

COLLOCATION 1

1 Match the nouns (1–8) to the nouns (a–h) to make collocations about transport.

1	traffic	**a**	transport
2	public	**b**	restrictions
3	cycle	**c**	charge
4	rush	**d**	congestion
5	car	**e**	lane
6	road	**f**	share
7	congestion	**g**	rage
8	parking	**h**	hour

2 Complete the sentences with collocations from Exercise 1.

1 _____ is a big problem in this city. The traffic jams are terrible.

2 I use _____ like trains or the underground to get to work.

3 You can't drive in the _____ . It's only for bicycles.

4 _____ stop anyone leaving their car here.

5 The _____ is usually from eight until nine in the morning.

6 I use a _____ programme and drive to work with a co-worker.

7 If people get too angry in a traffic jam, it's called

_____ .

8 You have to pay the _____ to drive into the city centre.

ACADEMIC SYNONYMS

3 Replace the verbs in bold (1–8) with their academic synonyms in the box.

> prevent   organize   select   attempt
> consider   convince   realize   require

1 We **need** more public transport in the city like a light rail network.

2 Commuters **try** to arrive on time but traffic often causes delays.

3 PRT passengers **choose** their destination from a digital menu.

4 The government needs to **understand** that the trains are too crowded.

5 We **run** a car share programme.

6 We should **think about** cycling instead of driving short distances.

7 New roads will **stop** traffic congestion in the short term.

8 It will be difficult to **get** drivers to use public transport.

CRITICAL THINKING

At the end of this unit, you will write a problem–solution essay. Look at this unit's Writing task in the box below.

> Describe the traffic problems in this city and outline the advantages and disadvantages of the suggested solutions. Which of the suggestions is most suitable?

ANALYZE

1 Work with a partner. Look at the map below, showing a city with serious traffic congestion problems. Discuss what the problems could be and make a list of at least three. One has been done for you as an example.

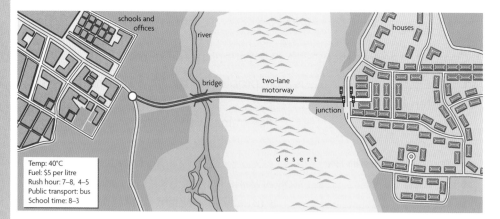

Problem 1

The residential area is on one side of the river and the economic centre and the schools are on the other side of the river. However, there is only one road into and out of the city centre.

Problem 2

_____
_____
_____
_____

Problem 3

_____
_____
_____
_____

Problem 4

_____
_____
_____
_____

2 Suggest a solution for each of the four traffic problems shown on the map, and make notes on the possible issues. The first one has been done for you as an example.

Solutions to traffic congestion	Possible issues
1 Building a tunnel	Expensive to build under the river Would fill with traffic eventually
2	
3	
4	

WRITING

GRAMMAR FOR WRITING

First conditional

We often use the first conditional to persuade or negotiate. Notice how we use *if* and *will* to link two sentences.

idea/action: The government increases tax on fuel.
consequence: People use their cars less.

If the government increases tax on fuel, people will use their cars less.

or

People will use their cars less, if the government increases tax on fuel.

idea/action: We build another bridge.
consequence: More traffic can get to the schools and offices.

If we build another bridge, more traffic will be able to get to the schools and offices.

1 Read the grammar explanation on page 79 and answer the questions below.

   1 Which clause begins with *if*?
   a the idea clause
   b the consequence clause
   2 Which clause contains *will*?
   a the idea clause
   b the consequence clause
   3 What happens to *can* when it follows *will* in a sentence?

2 Link the pairs of sentences below using *if* and *will*. Remember to change *can* in Question 5.

   1 We move the offices and schools next to the houses. We have fewer traffic problems.
   2 We have a ferry over the river. Fewer people use the bridge.
   3 Fewer cars use the roads. We increase the price of fuel.
   4 We change the office hours. The cars do not all use the road at the same time.
   5 We build a railway line. People can use the train instead of their cars.

Using *if ... not* and *unless*

We can also use *if ... not* or *unless* to describe the consequence of not doing a certain action.

idea/action: The government increases tax on fuel.
consequence: People use their cars less.

If the government **doesn't** increase tax on fuel, people **won't** use their cars less.
Unless the government increases tax on fuel, people **won't** use their cars less.

3 Link the sentences below using *if ... not* or *unless*.

   1 The traffic will improve. We build more roads.
   2 Pollution will be reduced. We use cleaner transport.
   3 We provide a solution. People will get to work on time.
   4 We will solve the traffic problem. We build houses closer to the business areas.
   5 The city invests in a PRT. There will be less congestion.

ACADEMIC WRITING SKILLS

Writing a conclusion

In an essay conclusion, we bring together all the points from the main body and state our personal opinion on the question. We then make a final comment to answer the question.

1 Match each main point (1–3) to a personal opinion (a–c) and a final comment (i–iii) to make three different conclusions.

1 In conclusion, this town's traffic problems are as a result of a single bridge over the river.

2 Overall, although there are a number of good solutions to the traffic problem, the main issue is housing.

3 To sum up, it is clear that the traffic congestion is a serious problem which will require a new approach to transport in the city.

a In my opinion, encouraging public transport is cheaper and more effective than building more bridges and roads.

b I would say that building houses next to the offices would solve this problem.

c It is my view that a new river crossing offers the best solution.

i Building more bridges will allow traffic freedom of movement between the two areas and perhaps charging drivers to use one of the bridges will help recover the costs.

ii Buses and trains will be able to solve the congestion problems and reduce the amount of traffic, which might also have a positive effect on the environment.

iii It is a long-term and expensive solution but relocating workers next to their offices should prevent traffic jams and allow people to walk to work.

2 Answer the questions.

1 What phrases are used to introduce the conclusions in Exercise 1?
2 What phrases are used to introduce opinions in Exercise 1?

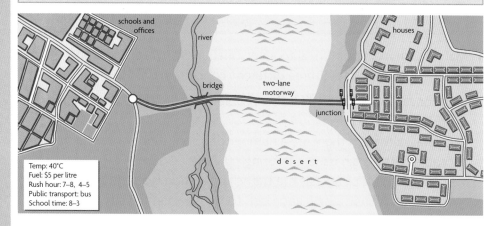

WRITING TASK

Describe the traffic problems in this city and outline the advantages and disadvantages of the suggested solutions. Which of the suggestions is most suitable?

schools and offices

river

houses

bridge

two-lane motorway

junction

desert

Temp: 40°C
Fuel: $5 per litre
Rush hour: 7–8, 4–5
Public transport: bus
School time: 8–3

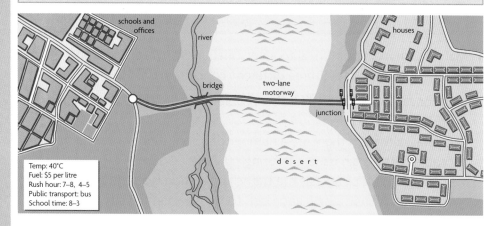

1 Look back at the problems and solutions you discussed in the Critical thinking section on page 78 and complete the essay plan below.

PLAN

Introduction

Solution 1: _____

Reasons: _____

Issues: _____

Solution 2: _____

Reasons: _____

Issues: _____

Solution 3: _____

Reasons: _____

Issues: _____

2 Respond to the task by writing three paragraphs about the solutions to the city's traffic problems, explaining the reasons for each solution and its disadvantages. Then write a conclusion, including your personal opinion.

> The map shows the traffic problems of a busy city.
>
> The city seems to have very bad traffic congestion. This makes people late, wastes fuel and adds to pollution in the city. People have to travel from their homes on one side of the river to their offices and schools on the other. The main problem is that there is only one main road running through the centre which takes all the car traffic, and only one bridge. The only public transport is a bus which also uses the same road. There is also a junction near the housing area where the traffic builds up during the two rush hours, when people commute to work or drop off their children at school.

---

3 Use the task checklist to review your essay for content and structure.

TASK CHECKLIST	✔
Are there three solution paragraphs in the main body, and have you evaluated the different solutions by giving reasons?	
Does your conclusion summarize the main body, give your opinion and answer the question?	
Have you included enough data from the diagram to support your opinion?	

4 Make any necessary changes to your essay.

5 Now use the language checklist to edit your essay for language errors which are common to B1 learners.

LANGUAGE CHECKLIST	✔
Have you replaced general verbs with academic words where possible?	
Have you used *if, will, unless* and *if … not* correctly?	
Have you used *in conclusion, to sum up* or *overall* to introduce your conclusion?	

6 Make any necessary changes to your essay.

OBJECTIVES REVIEW

7 Check your objectives.

I can ...

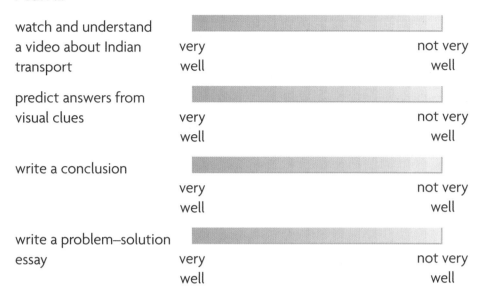

	very well	not very well
watch and understand a video about Indian transport		
predict answers from visual clues		
write a conclusion		
write a problem–solution essay		

WORDLIST

UNIT VOCABULARY	ACADEMIC VOCABULARY
bus lane (n)	attempt (v)
carbon-neutral (adj)	consider (v)
congestion charge (n)	convince (v)
outskirts (n)	issue (n)
public transport (n)	major (adj)
roadrage (n)	prevent (v)
run (v)	realize (v)
rush hour (n)	require (v)
traffic congestion (n)	select (v)
vandalism (n)	
vehicle (n)	

LEARNING OBJECTIVES

Watch and listen	Watch and understand a video about global warming
Reading skills	Scan to find detailed pieces of information quickly
Academic writing skills	Write a topic sentence
Writing task	Write two cause–effect paragraphs

UNLOCK YOUR KNOWLEDGE

Work with a partner. Discuss the questions below.

1 Is the weather changing in your country?
2 How have humans affected the environment?
3 Why should we care about the environment?

WATCH AND LISTEN

PREPARING TO WATCH

USING YOUR KNOWLEDGE TO PREDICT CONTENT

1 You are going to watch a video about glaciers. Before you watch, discuss the questions below with a partner.

1 What is a glacier?
2 Where can you find glaciers?
3 What is happening to the glacier in the photographs?
4 What do you think is the cause of the changes to the glacier?

UNDERSTANDING KEY VOCABULARY

2 Match the words and phrases (1–6) to their definitions (a–f).

1 a glacier	**a** the air, water and land in or on which people, animals and plants live
2 the environment	
3 an ice sheet	**b** a gradual increase in world temperatures
4 global warming	**c** a river caused by melting ice
5 a melt stream	**d** a large mass of ice which moves slowly
6 a transformation	**e** a complete change in the appearance or character of something
	f a thick layer of frozen water that permanently covers an area of land

WHILE WATCHING

UNDERSTANDING MAIN IDEAS

3 ▶ Watch the video. Complete the summary using the words and phrases in the box.

> melt   environment   effects   global warming   formed   glaciers

The video is about the Alaskan (1)_____ . The speaker explains how they are (2)_____ and what causes them to (3)_____ . He talks about the (4)_____ of melting glaciers and blames (5)_____ for the changes to the (6)_____ .

4 ▶ Watch again and complete the diagram below.

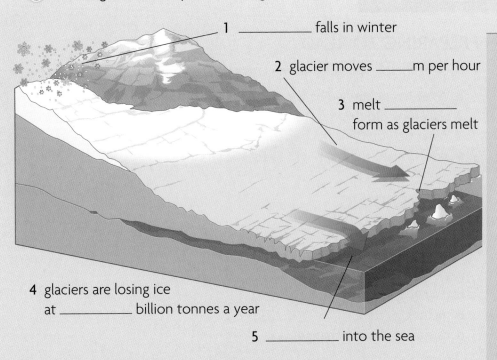

1 _____ falls in winter

2 glacier moves _____m per hour

3 melt _____
form as glaciers melt

4 glaciers are losing ice
at _____ billion tonnes a year

5 _____ into the sea

5 Work with a partner. Try to answer the questions below.

1 The speaker says that every glacier is in balance – if it is not in balance, it will melt. The glaciers are melting, so what part of the balance is wrong?
2 Does the video claim that humans are responsible for the glacier melting?
3 How long have the Alaskan glaciers been there?

DISCUSSION

6 Work with a partner. Discuss the questions below and give reasons for your answers.

1 Do you think climate change is the result of human activity?
2 Whose responsibility is it to try to stop the climate changing?
3 What steps can companies and governments take to reduce the problems of climate change?
4 What steps can you take individually to help to protect the environment?

PREPARING TO READ

USING YOUR
KNOWLEDGE TO
PREDICT CONTENT

1 Look at the photographs of the Upsala glacier and answer the questions.

    1 What has happened to the glacier?

    2 How long did this transformation take?

    3 What do you think happened to the water?

    4 How do you think this will affect the world?

WHILE READING

READING FOR
MAIN IDEAS

UNL**O**CK
ONLINE

2 Read the leaflet and number the main ideas (a–d) in the order that they are mentioned.

    a a solution to the problem _____

    b changing ecosystems   _____

    c melting glaciers   _____

    d causes of climate change _____

SCANNING TO FIND
INFORMATION

3 Complete the sentences below using the words and phrases in the box.

> mangrove forests   agriculture   global sea levels   extinction
> global temperatures   coral reefs CO_2 levels

    1 _____ are at their highest for 800,000 years.

    2 _____ could rise by about 59 centimetres by the end of the century.

    3 Recently, over 33% of the world's _____ have been destroyed.

    4 Over the last century, _____ have gone up by 0.75 degrees.

    5 Twenty-five percent of the land on earth is used for

    _____ .

    6 Global increases in temperature could cause the _____ of 30% of land species.

    7 Twenty percent of _____ have been lost in the last few decades.

Scanning to find information

Scanning is a good way to find detailed pieces of information quickly. Many examinations test your comprehension of figures. It is a good idea to underline all the figures in the questions and then scan the text for each specific figure. When you find the figure in the text, look at the words around it for the answer to the question.

Our changing planet

1928

2004

The Upsala glacier in Argentina used to be one of the biggest glaciers in South America. In 1928, it was covered in ice and snow but now the glacier is melting at an annual rate of 200 metres, so the area is covered in water. This is evidence of global warming.

In the last 100 years, the global temperature has gone up by around 0.75 degrees Celsius. This may not sound much but such a small increase is causing sea levels to rise and threatening the habitat of many species of plants and animals. An increase of two degrees Celsius in global temperatures could result in extinction for 30% of the world's land species.

The Northwest Passage is a sea route which runs along the northern coast of Canada between the Atlantic and the Pacific Oceans. In the past, it was often difficult to use, as the waters were frozen; however, increasing temperatures and the subsequent deglaciation have made it easier to travel down this route. The major issue is that this will lead to loss of habitat for the polar bears and other species that live in this area.

Sea levels in the UK have increased by around 10 cm in the last 100 years and experts predict that global sea levels could rise by up to 59 cm by the end of the century. Consequently, areas which were land a few hundred years ago are now submerged and many low-lying islands may be under water in the future.

As a result of the changing climate, the world's ecosystems are also changing faster than ever before. Over one-third of the world's mangrove forests and around 20% of the world's coral reefs have been destroyed in the last few decades. Forests are being cut down to provide land for food because the population is growing at such a rapid rate. Approximately a quarter of land on earth is now used agriculturally for growing food. As a result of the higher temperatures and higher levels of carbon dioxide in the atmosphere, plants are producing more pollen which could lead to more cases of asthma.

So what is causing climate change? The main cause of climate change is the huge amount of greenhouse gases such as methane and carbon dioxide (CO_2) in the atmosphere, but the reason for this is the world's population – you and me. As the population increases, more land is needed to provide food, and more energy is needed. Burning fossil fuels for heating, lighting, transport, electricity or manufacturing produces CO_2. Furthermore, humans breathe out CO_2 and trees 'breathe in' CO_2 and produce oxygen – so by cutting down trees, we are increasing the amount of CO_2 in the atmosphere and reducing the amount of oxygen. As a result of these activities, CO_2 levels are now at their highest for 800,000 years.

The biggest challenge we all face is to prevent further environmental disasters. We must do something before it is too late. We need to reduce the amount of CO_2 in the atmosphere. We need to stop burning fossil fuels and start using renewable energy. We can get enough energy from renewable fuels like solar energy, hydroelectric energy or wind power to be able to stop using fossil fuels completely.

Sign the petition to get governments to take action before it is too late!

4 Look at the leaflet again and answer the questions below in no more than three words.

1 In which country is the Upsala glacier?

_____

2 What is the name of the 'new' sea route through the arctic ice?

_____

3 Many forests are being cut down all over the world. What is the land needed for?

_____

4 What medical problem could more pollen production lead to?

_____

5 What is the term for the main chemicals responsible for climate change?

_____

6 What do humans do that reduces the amount of oxygen in the atmosphere?

_____

7 What should governments start using to reduce the amount of CO_2 in the atmosphere?

_____

READING BETWEEN THE LINES

5 Why did the author write the leaflet?

a To inform the reader about the causes and effects of climate change
b To educate the reader about how to stop climate change
c To convince people to sign a petition about using renewable fuels

DISCUSSION

6 Work with a partner. Discuss the questions below.

1 Are there any advantages to the 'new' Northwest Passage?
2 Are there any disadvantages to using renewable energy like solar energy or wind power?
3 Why don't governments, corporations and individuals do more to help prevent global warming?

READING 2

PREPARING TO READ

1 Look at the photograph and the title of the journal extract on page 94 and try to answer the questions below.

   1 Why are trees important to the environment?
   2 Why do people cut down trees?
   3 What will happen when we destroy too many trees?

2 Match the words and phrases (1–9) to their definitions (a–i).

1	flooding	a	when all the trees in a large area are cut down
2	erosion	b	when animals feed on grass or plants
3	deforestation	c	the number and types of plant and animal species that exist in a particular area
4	subsistence farming	d	when an area is covered in water
5	absorb	e	cutting down trees for wood
6	biodiversity	f	cattle or other farm animals
7	logging	g	farming that only provides enough food for farmers and their families to live on
8	grazing	h	to take something in, especially gradually
9	livestock	i	gradual damage and removal of soil, stone, etc., by the sea, rain, or wind

WHILE READING

3 Read the journal extract on page 94 and complete the summary below using the words in the box.

> livestock   erosion   environment   fires   crops   effects
> deforestation   decade   habitats   protected

The essay discusses the human causes of (1)_____ and the (2)_____ on the environment. Trees are removed for grazing of (3)_____ and growing (4)_____ like soya and palm oil. Subsistence farmers traditionally leave the land for a (5)_____ before reusing it but if the land is constantly reused, it results in (6)_____ of the soil. Deforestation contributes to global warming because it dries out the trees, causing forest (7)_____ . It affects biodiversity because it leads to the loss of (8)_____ . Governments should make sure forests are (9)_____ from logging. Deforestation will have terrible consequences for the (10)_____ .

Deforestation means the removal of a forest so that the land is converted for urban use or agriculture. The destruction of forests occurs for many reasons: trees are used as fuel or for construction, while cleared land is used as pasture for livestock and crop plantations. The main adverse effects of deforestation are aridity and damage to animal habitat, as well as climate change and erosion damage.

The main causes of deforestation are commercial agriculture by big business and subsistence farming by local people. In Indonesia, industrial logging is carried out to clear areas for the production of palm oil while in Brazil, large areas of the Amazon rainforest were cleared to grow soya and vegetable oil. Subsistence farmers clear an area big enough to graze cattle or grow crops by cutting down the trees and burning them. However, after two or three years, the land can no longer be used so the farmer moves to another piece of land. It takes around ten years for the piece of land to recover. However, in populated areas, the land cannot recover and this leads to heavy erosion because the layer of soil that protects the ground is removed during the crop-growing process. This can cause flooding problems in heavy rain.

One area affected by deforestation is the Amazon Basin in Brazil. The vast rainforests of the Amazon cover an area around 25 times the size of the UK and absorb an estimated 1.5 billion tonnes of carbon dioxide annually. They are thought to have helped keep global warming under control in recent years. However, in areas where deforestation has taken place, the increased temperatures result in less rain because there are not enough trees to provide water for clouds to form. If tropical forests dry out, more trees will die and there will be more logging and more fires. This will cause more emissions of carbon dioxide, making the rainforest contribute to global warming rather than help solve it.

Forest destruction is also having an effect on biodiversity. The growth in the world's population is causing the loss of habitats and damage to land where plants and animal species live, reducing biodiversity and leading to the extinction of many species. A decrease in biodiversity threatens entire ecosystems and destroys future sources of food and medicine.

The damage caused by humans to the world's forests leads to changes in the natural environment and causes global warming. Governments should act to protect forests from illegal logging and plant more trees to absorb carbon dioxide. Deforestation on such a large scale is sure to have disastrous effects for the environment.

WHAT ARE THE CAUSES OF

deforestation

AND WHAT ARE ITS EFFECTS ON THE natural environment?

4 Correct the factual mistakes in the sentences.

1 In Indonesia, trees are cut down to make way for olive oil plantations.

2 Subsistence farmers can graze livestock on their land for ten years.

3 The rainforests of the Amazon cover an area 25 times the size of the USA.

4 Deforestation protects future sources of food and medicine.

5 Governments should plant more trees to absorb oxygen.

6 Small-scale deforestation will have disastrous effects for the environment.

READING BETWEEN THE LINES

5 Work with a partner. Try to answer the questions below.

1 What does the writer mean by the phrases *industrial logging* and *commercial agriculture?*
2 Why will there be more logging if forests dry out?
3 Why does deforestation reduce future sources of food and medicine?

DISCUSSION

6 Work with a partner. Discuss the questions below.

1 If a product, service or behaviour is designed not to do harm to the environment, we say it is 'environmentally friendly'. Do you think you are environmentally friendly? Why / Why not?
2 What measures could governments take to stop humans damaging the natural environment?
3 What is the most important environmental problem in your country?

◉ LANGUAGE DEVELOPMENT

ACADEMIC VOCABULARY

1 Replace the underlined words in the sentences below with the academic words in the box.

> annual   issue   predict   challenge   areas   trend   consequences

1 The most serious <u>problem</u> that threatens the environment is climate change. _____

2 Experts <u>think</u> that there will not be enough fresh water in the future. _____

3 Pollution and climate change are the <u>effects</u> of human activity. _____

4 Fortunately, the <u>pattern</u> is for more recycling and less packaging. _____

5 In some <u>places</u>, the glaciers have melted or even disappeared as a result of higher temperatures. _____

6 The <u>twelve-month</u> rate of deforestation between 1990 and 2005 was around seven to eight million hectares. _____

7 The biggest <u>test</u> we face is to protect the planet. _____

TOPIC VOCABULARY

2 Complete the collocations related to the environment by adding the missing vowels. Look back at the reading texts if you need help.

1 If we change to r__n__w__bl__ __n__rgy instead of using f__ss__l f__ __ls, we can reduce CO_2 in the atmosphere.

2 Gl__b__l w__rm__ng is caused by the increase in gr__ __nh__ __s__ g__s__s in the atmosphere.

3 The n__t__r__l __nv__r__nm__nt is being affected by h__m__n __ct__v__ty.

4 D__f__r__st__t__ __n caused by cutting down trees is leading to cl__m__t__ ch__ng__ .

5 Illegal l__gg__ng is having a serious effect on the Amazonian r__ __nf__r__st.

6 S__bs__st__nc__ f__rm__ng in rainforests causes damage to the soil.

7 We must take action to prevent any more __nv__r__nm__nt__l d__s__st__rs.

CRITICAL THINKING

At the end of this unit, you will write two cause–effect paragraphs. Look at this unit's Writing task in the box below.

> Outline the human causes of climate change. What effects will these have on the planet?

Selecting

When you do research for an essay, you need to select which information will be useful for the different parts of your essay. To do this you must constantly think about your essay title and ask yourself whether the information is relevant or not.

Work in pairs and do tasks 1–3 below.

EVALUATE

1 Decide which points in the box are causes of climate change and which ones are the effects, and complete the ideas maps below.

> melting glaciers   storms   rising sea levels
> factory emissions   deforestation   petrol cars   loss of habitat
> species extinction   flooding   increase in the population
> droughts   power stations   livestock

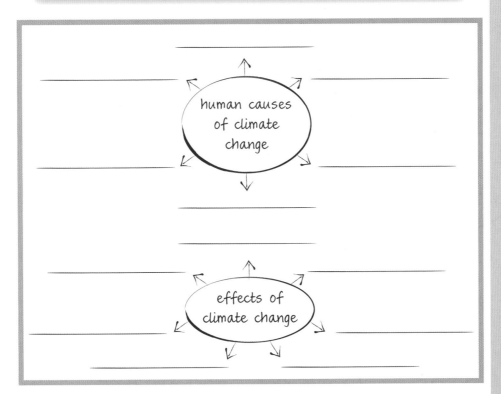

2 Now add some of your own ideas to the ideas maps.
3 Discuss possible solutions to this problem.

WRITING

GRAMMAR FOR WRITING

EXPLANATION

Cause and effect

When we write a 'cause and effect' essay, we need certain phrases to show the relationship between the causes of the problem and its effects. Look at the sentences below.

cause	linking word or phrase	effect
Deforestation	leads to causes results in	habitat destruction.

effect	linking word or phrase	cause
Habitat destruction is	caused by due to the result of	deforestation.

UNLOCK ONLINE

1 Using the information from your ideas maps in the Critical thinking section on page 97, complete the flow charts by adding linking words. More than one answer is possible. The first one has been done for you as an example.

Global warming (1) _____leads to_____ higher temperatures, and (2) _____ melting glaciers.	Melting glaciers are (3) _____ higher temperatures, which are (4) _____ global warming.

2 Complete the sentences using one linking word.

1 Deforestation _____ in animal extinction and loss of biodiversity.

2 Demand for food and energy are expected to rise _____ to the increase in the population.

3 Burning fossil fuels _____ an increase in CO_2 in the atmosphere.

4 Flooding, heat waves and other extreme weather are all _____ by climate change.

5 Reducing livestock on farms may _____ in lower greenhouse gas emissions.

6 Submerged islands could be the _____ of rising sea levels.

7 Droughts will _____ to forest fires and further emission of carbon dioxide.

Using *because* and *because of*

because is a conjunction that introduces a reason. This usually contains a subject, a verb and an object.

The environment is changing **because** humans are burning fossil fuels.

because of is a two-word preposition meaning *as a result of*. It is followed by a noun phrase (made up of articles, adjectives and nouns).

The climate is changing **because of** human activity.

3 Complete the sentences using *because* or *because of*.

1 Rising sea levels are a potential problem _____ flooding.

2 A loss of biodiversity will be problematic _____ it will limit new sources of food and medicine.

3 Humans are the cause of climate change _____ deforestation and burning fossil fuels.

4 Low-lying islands may be submerged _____ rising sea levels.

5 Animal extinction rates are increasing _____ habitat is being destroyed.

6 People are now more interested in climate change _____ recent droughts.

7 The climate is changing _____ human activity.

ACADEMIC WRITING SKILLS

EXPLANATION

Topic sentences

A topic sentence is usually the first sentence in a paragraph. It introduces the topic of the paragraph and links back to the main topic of the essay. We can use a general statement, or we can include the topics of the supporting sentences. Notice that both kinds of topic sentence refer to the <u>main essay topic</u>.

Using a general statement

a <u>Human activity is causing the environment to change</u> in a number of ways.

b <u>The environment is changing</u> in three main ways.

Including the topics of the supporting sentences

c <u>Humans are the cause of climate change</u> because of **deforestation** and **burning fossil fuels**.

d **Rising temperatures, loss of biodiversity** and **rising sea levels** are <u>the main results of climate change</u>.

1 Look at the topic sentences (a–d) in the box above and answer the questions.

   1 Which sentences introduce paragraphs about the causes of climate change? _____

   2 Which sentences introduce paragraphs about the effects of climate change? _____

   3 How many supporting sentences will the paragraph for sentence c have? _____

   4 How many supporting sentences will the paragraph for sentence d have? _____

2 Complete the sentences using ideas from the Critical thinking section on page 97 and information in the box above.

   1 _____ , _____ and _____ are the most obvious causes of climate change.

   2 There are many effects of climate change including _____ and _____ .

   3 The environment is being affected in _____ .

   4 _____ and _____ will probably be the main results of a change in the climate.

   5 Humans are to blame for changing the climate in _____ .

WRITING TASK

Outline the human causes of climate change. What effects will these have on the planet?

1 Read the introduction and conclusion below. Then write two paragraphs: one about the human causes of climate change and another about the effects.

Human activity is having a major effect on the environment, which will cause many problems for human and animal life in the future. This essay will set out the main causes of climate change and the effects of human activity on the environment.

_____

_____

_____

_____

_____

_____

_____

_____

_____

_____

_____

_____

_____

_____

_____

_____

_____

_____

_____

_____

_____

_____

Human activity is clearly causing the climate to change and, as a result, this is having a number of effects on the planet. It is important that we try to reduce our negative impact on the planet as much as possible – for example, by using renewable energy instead of fossil fuels – before it is too late.

2 Use the task checklist to review your paragraphs for content and structure.

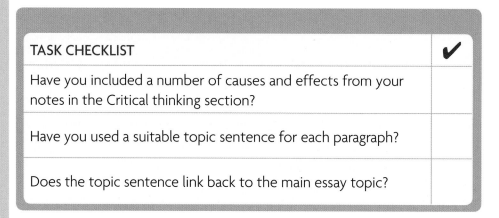

TASK CHECKLIST	✔
Have you included a number of causes and effects from your notes in the Critical thinking section?	
Have you used a suitable topic sentence for each paragraph?	
Does the topic sentence link back to the main essay topic?	

3 Make any necessary changes to your paragraphs.

4 Now use the language checklist to edit your paragraphs for language errors which are common to B1 learners.

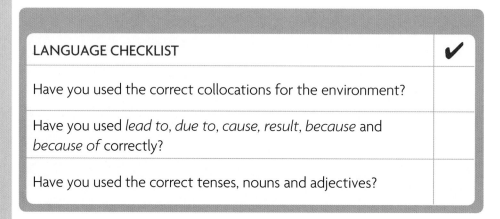

LANGUAGE CHECKLIST	✔
Have you used the correct collocations for the environment?	
Have you used *lead to*, *due to*, *cause*, *result*, *because* and *because of* correctly?	
Have you used the correct tenses, nouns and adjectives?	

5 Make any necessary changes to your paragraphs.

OBJECTIVES REVIEW

6 Check your objectives.

I can ...

watch and understand a video about global warming	very well · not very well
scan to find detailed pieces of information quickly	very well · not very well
write a topic sentence	very well · not very well
write two cause–effect paragraphs	very well · not very well

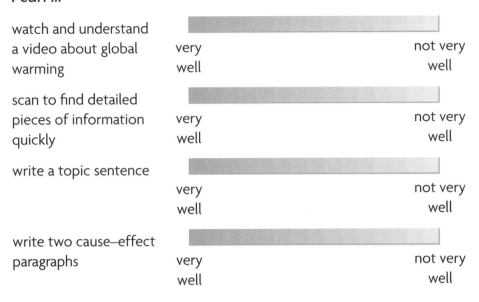

WORDLIST

UNIT VOCABULARY	ACADEMIC VOCABULARY
biodiversity (n)	annual (adj)
climate change (n)	area (n)
consequence (n)	cause (v)
deforestation (n)	challenge (n)
drought (n)	decade (n)
emission (n)	effect (n)
erosion (n)	issue (n)
flood (n)	the environment (n)
fossil fuel (n)	trend (n)
glacier (n)	predict (v)
global warming (n)	
graze (v)	
greenhouse gas (n)	
submerge (v)	
subsistence farming (n)	

LEARNING OBJECTIVES

Watch and listen	Watch and understand a video about professional cyclists
Reading skills	Read for detail
Academic writing skills	Write supporting sentences
Writing task	Write a problem–solution essay

UNL⌀CK YOUR KNOWLEDGE

1 Match the two halves of these phrases.

1	avoid	a	some exercise
2	keep	b	on fat, salt and sugar
3	eat	c	more fruit and vegetables
4	lose	d	weight
5	cut down	e	cigarettes and alcohol
6	take	f	active

2 Answer the questions.

1 Do you agree with the advice given in the sentences above?

2 Why do doctors advise us to look after our health?

3 Should doctors treat illnesses in people who have not looked after their health?

WATCH AND LISTEN

PREPARING TO WATCH

USING YOUR KNOWLEDGE TO PREDICT CONTENT

1 Answer the questions below.

1 What makes a good professional sportsperson?
2 How do professional sportspeople get an advantage over their competitors?

UNDERSTANDING KEY VOCABULARY

2 Complete the sentences by making collocations about fitness using the verbs in the box.

> generate   burn   set   extract   pump

1 When you breathe, you _____ (take away) oxygen from the air and you breathe out carbon dioxide.
2 Moving your arms and legs makes the heart _____ (push) blood to the muscles.
3 If you want to achieve something, you can _____ (decide on) goals to help you.
4 You need to _____ (use up) fat if you want to lose weight.
5 If you train efficiently, you can _____ (produce) more power from the same amount of energy.

WHILE WATCHING

UNDERSTANDING MAIN IDEAS

3 ▶ Watch the video and circle the points (a–i) that are discussed.

a French cyclists
b training routine
c medical problems
d ability to generate energy
e the team

f the support vehicle
g sponsors
h equipment
i diet

4 ▶ Watch again and complete the notes about professional cyclists.

Top road cyclists

Ride (1)_____ kilometres in each race at a speed of

(2)_____ kilometres per hour.

Fitness

The best riders extract twice as much (3)_____ from
every breath as a normal person.

Heart pumps (4)_____ gallons of blood

Normal person pumps (5)_____ gallons of blood

Team

Their job is to block the (6)_____

Equipment

Use (7)_____ technology for bike

Bike weight: (8)_____

In the Tour de France, riders eat (9)_____ calories in
carbohydrates daily

---

5 Work with a partner. Try to answer the questions below.

  1 How are professional cyclists able to ride so far and so fast?
  2 The best riders use a wind tunnel to analyze their body positions.
     Why?
  3 Why do professional cyclists ride in a team?

DISCUSSION

6 Work with a partner. Discuss the questions below.

  1 How difficult is it to become a professional sportsperson?
  2 Which professional sports are popular in your country?
  3 Are professional sportspeople good role models for young people?

PREPARING TO READ

1 Match the words and phrases (1–8) to the definitions (a–h).

1 physical activity   **a** major medical problem
2 heart rate   **b** make a problem less likely
3 serious illness   **c** scientific proof
4 medical evidence   **d** exercise
5 reduce the risk of   **e** how fast your heart pumps
6 self-esteem   **f** working with your hands
7 chronic disease   **g** long-lasting disease
8 manual labour   **h** how you feel about yourself

2 Name the types of exercise shown in the photographs.

1 _____

2 _____

3 _____

4 _____

5 _____

6 _____

7 _____

8 _____

KEEP FIT!

IT'S EASIER THAN YOU MIGHT THINK.

A How much physical activity do you do in a week? Are you getting enough exercise? People who do regular activity have a lower risk of many chronic diseases, such as heart disease, type 2 diabetes, stroke and some cancers. Adults who do exercise for just 150 minutes a week can reduce their risk of serious illness by 50%. Regular exercise reduces the risk of early death by 30%. It also improves your mood, self-esteem and sleep quality. Today, we are much less active than in the past and our office jobs are far less physical than the manual labour our grandfathers used to do. In fact, many adults spend seven hours or more on a chair each day.

B This lack of regular physical activity means that people burn fewer calories than in the past, so we need to do something extra to use up all our energy. Adults need to do two and a half hours of moderate exercise per week. This could be fast walking or cycling on a flat road. In addition, you should do exercise to strengthen muscles twice a week.

C Exercise can be expensive, but it doesn't have to be. Team sports such as football, rugby or cricket can be cheap because all the players share the cost of the pitch. Joining a sports club is usually a cheap way of getting exercise and can be very sociable, too. Local leisure centres usually offer squash at cheap rates if you book a court at off-peak times, and you may be able to get cheap gym membership too. If the leisure centre has a pool, swimming is also a great way to exercise.

D Alternatively, if you don't want to spend any money at all, go for a run. The only equipment needed for this is a pair of trainers. Similarly, getting off the bus one stop early and walking the extra distance helps. Go to the park. Try getting a group of friends or family together and have a game of football in the park or play the sorts of running games you haven't played since you were a child. This is a great way to spend time with the family but also to help you get fit again. Alternatively, if you want to stay at home, gardening or doing housework is a great way to get fit and you can enjoy the benefit of a nice garden and a tidy house, too!

E Although adults should do two and a half hours of exercise a week, you don't have to do it all at one time. Split the time into ten-minute chunks! If you do ten minutes before work, ten minutes during your lunch break and ten minutes after work, five days a week, you've achieved the target! Alternatively, go swimming during your lunch hour two or three times a week and you've done it! There are many ways of getting fit and we should all recognize the value of doing this, because we will live longer and be more healthy.

WHILE READING

3 Skim the text. What type of text is it?

a an essay   b a report   c a leaflet   d a letter

SKIMMING

4 Match the headings (1–6) to the paragraphs in the text (A–E). There is one extra heading which you do not need.

1 But I can't afford gym membership!

2 150 minutes a week is all it takes!

3 But I don't have time!

4 Swimming is the best form of exercise.

5 Burn that extra energy!

6 Exercise can be free.

5 Read the text and answer the questions.

1 Which four medical problems can be avoided by regular exercise?

2 Which three things does exercise improve?

3 How much time do some adults spend each day sitting down?

4 What do team sport players share the cost of?

5 When should you book a squash court for cheap rates?

6 What equipment do you need for running?

7 Where should you go to exercise and spend time with your family?

8 What should we all recognize the value of?

6 Complete the phrases using words from the text to describe ways of getting fit. The first one has been done for you as an example.

1 use up   _energy_

2 burn   _____

3 strengthen   _____

4 join   _____

5 book   _____

6 go for   _____

7 get off   _____

8 live   _____

7 Answer the questions.

1 How many different ways to get fit are mentioned in the text?

2 What are they?

READING BETWEEN THE LINES

8 Try to answer the questions below.

1 What have you achieved if you go swimming during your lunch hour two or three times a week?

2 How does exercise improve self-esteem?

3 Why are leisure activities cheaper at off-peak times?

4 Is the leaflet written for adults or for children? How do you know?

DISCUSSION

9 Work with a partner. Discuss the questions below.

1 How do you keep fit?

2 Is doing sport the best way to keep fit? Why / Why not?

3 What problems are associated with doing too much exercise?

READING 2

PREPARING TO READ

1 Work with a partner. Try to answer the questions below.

1 What percentage of your diet should be
   a fruit and vegetables?
   b carbohydrates?
   c dairy products?
   d proteins?
2 How do countries help people avoid obesity?

2 Scan the essay on page 112 and check your answers to the questions.

USING YOUR
KNOWLEDGE TO
PREDICT CONTENT

WHILE READING

3 Read the essay in more detail. Which paragraphs contain the themes (1–6) below?

1 a tax on certain foods _____
2 the importance of the government's role _____
3 a healthy diet _____
4 nutritional value _____
5 an introduction to the subject _____
6 advertising _____

READING FOR
MAIN IDEAS

4 Read paragraphs B–E again and make notes on why the author suggests these solutions to the problem of obesity.

ways to tackle obesity	reason
a balanced diet (paragraph B)	1 _____ _____
packaging labels (paragraph C)	2 _____ _____
a food tax (paragraph D)	3 _____ _____
a ban on junk food advertising (paragraph E)	4 _____ _____
education campaigns (paragraph E)	5 _____ _____

Tackling obesity

A Obesity is becoming a major problem in many parts of the world. In Britain alone, there was a 30% increase in the number of people being admitted to hospital with problems related to obesity last year. An estimated 60% of British adults are overweight.

B One way of tackling obesity is to eat less but to eat more healthily. An average man needs around 2,500 calories per day, while an average woman requires around 2,000 per day. We should eat a balanced diet which consists of a variety of foods in order to maintain a healthy weight. A healthy diet should include approximately 35% fruit and vegetables; 35% carbohydrates, such as bread, rice, potatoes and pasta (or other starchy food); around 15% dairy products like milk and cheese; 10% proteins, for example meat, fish, eggs and beans; and only around 5% should be sweet foods – namely cakes or biscuits – especially those that are high in fat and sugar.

C In many countries, nutritional values are shown on food packaging. In Britain, there is a traffic light system to show more clearly how good or bad a particular food product is. Red next to 'sugar', for example, means that the product is high in that particular item; yellow means the product is neither high nor low in sugar; and green means the product only has a small amount of sugar in it. The traffic light system helps people to know immediately whether the food product is good for them.

D Some people argue that foods that are high in fat, such as pizza and potato chips, and those high in refined sugar, like chocolate and sweets, should be taxed. This would make junk food too expensive for people to buy in large quantities. In Denmark, there is now a tax on products that contain more than 2.3% of saturated fat. However, taxing fast food is difficult because fast food companies are rich and powerful.

E The role of advertising should not be forgotten. Advertising junk food at times when children are watching TV was banned in Malaysia in 2007. This was designed to better protect them from the influence of advertising while they learn how to choose between treats and foods that are good for them. On the other hand, there have also been TV education campaigns to encourage people to eat five portions of fruit and vegetables per day. It has been estimated that if people ate enough fruit and vegetables, up to 2.7 million lives per year could be saved.

F Governments need to promote healthy eating and the importance of five portions of fruit and vegetables per day. Similarly, they need to fight obesity by discouraging people from eating fats and sugars. They must also encourage people to be more active by providing opportunities for everyone to get fit, no matter how rich or poor they may be. If governments can change people's habits, the world will be a healthier place in the future.

Reading for detail

Reading for detail means reading the text carefully to extract important details which help with understanding the text.

5 Read the essay again to look for the examples that the author uses to add detail to the argument.

topic	examples
1 carbohydrates	bread
2 dairy products	
3 proteins	
4 sweet foods	
5 high-fat foods	
6 sugary foods	

READING BETWEEN THE LINES

6 Work with a partner. Try to answer the questions below.

1 Why are governments interested in fighting obesity?
2 Apart from maintaining a healthy weight, why should we eat a variety of different types of food?
3 Many obese people in the UK are from poor areas. Why do you think this is?

DISCUSSION

7 Work with a partner. Discuss the questions below.

1 Is obesity a problem in your country?
2 Is your government doing anything to promote a healthy diet?
3 Do you agree that governments should charge a tax on products that are bad for our health? Why / Why not?

⊙ LANGUAGE DEVELOPMENT

Academic verbs and nouns

It is important to recognize both the verb and the noun form of academic words when you are reading, and to spell them correctly when you are writing.

1 Look at the verbs in the table and find their noun forms in the paragraph below. Write the nouns in the table next to the verb forms.

verb	noun
injure	1 _____
provide	2 _____
reduce	3 _____
suffer	4 _____
encourage	5 _____
solve	6 _____
recognize	7 _____
involve	8 _____

Children need to do more sport. We need to see a reduction in the rate of obesity and the suffering and injury it causes young people. The main solution is the increased provision of sports in schools. We also require the involvement and encouragement of parents, who are our main weapon against increasing obesity. The first step is recognition that fat is a real problem for young people.

COLLOCATION 2

2 Look at the short text below and underline ten collocations (noun + noun or adjective + noun) related to health and fitness. The first one has been done for you as an example.

Obesity can reduce <u>life expectancy</u> and lead to serious illness such as heart disease and diabetes. To address this problem, some governments run educational programmes and advertising campaigns. These educate people about the dangers of junk food and the importance of a balanced diet. They also show people how to find out about the nutritional value of food. Another important way to tackle obesity is regular exercise, because the more physical activity we have, the better we feel.

3 Now complete the table below by writing the correct collocation next to the definition.

definition	collocation
how long a person can expect to live	1 _life expectancy_
how good a particular kind of food is for you	2 _____
classes or material to teach people about a particular topic	3 _____
an illness of the heart	4 _____
moving around and doing things	5 _____
projects to convince people to buy a product or change their behaviour	6 _____
a very bad medical problem	7 _____
a mixture of the correct types and amounts of food	8 _____
sport or movement which people do at the same time each day, week, month, etc.	9 _____
food that is unhealthy but is quick and easy to eat	10 _____

CRITICAL THINKING

At the end of this unit, you will write a problem–solution essay. Look at this unit's Writing task in the box below.

> What can people do to live longer? What can a government do to increase the average life expectancy of its country's citizens?

Subdividing arguments

When we plan an essay, we make a list of our arguments. We can then subdivide them to allow us to better organize our essay.

1 Look at the ways we can increase life expectancy and decide which are about exercise (E) and which are about diet (D). The first one has been done for you as an example.

a do sports in parks and sports centres ___E___
b invest in school sports _____
c eat healthily _____
d tax junk food _____
e do regular exercise _____
f cut your calorie intake _____
g ban advertising of unhealthy food _____
h take advantage of free sports clubs for children _____
i fund national sports teams and athletes _____
j avoid salty food _____
k keep active with gardening and housework _____
l educate children about healthy food _____
m build more sports centres _____

2 Complete the chart using the arguments (a–m) above. Decide whether the arguments refer to individuals or to governments.

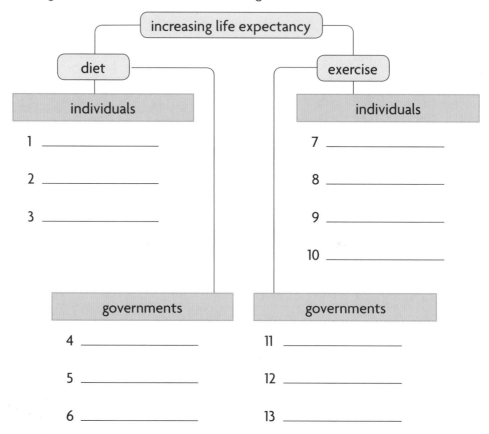

increasing life expectancy

diet — exercise

individuals

1 _____

2 _____

3 _____

individuals

7 _____

8 _____

9 _____

10 _____

governments

4 _____

5 _____

6 _____

governments

11 _____

12 _____

13 _____

WRITING

GRAMMAR FOR WRITING

Giving reasons

When we give reasons for our arguments, we can use *to* or *in order to*. Both are followed by an infinitive verb.

Governments should promote healthy eating	to	increase life expectancy.
	in order to	

We also use *so* or *so that*. This is followed by a clause with *can*.

Governments should build more sports centres	so	people can do more sports.
	so that	

1 Complete the sentences below using to, in order to, so or so that. More than one answer is possible.

1 Governments need to increase the tax on junk food _____ make it more expensive.

2 Nutrition labels should be added to packaging _____ people can see how healthy their food is.

3 Governments should provide free sports clubs _____ people from poorer backgrounds can take part in sport.

4 Governments can promote the idea of eating five portions of fruit and vegetables per day _____ improve people's diets.

5 It might be a good idea to tax unhealthy food _____ make it too expensive to buy a lot of it.

6 Some people argue that the junk food advertising should be banned _____ children are not influenced by it.

Giving examples

It is important to add detail to your writing by adding examples. It helps to give the reader more information and adds strength to your argument.

2 Complete the sentences below using the words and phrases in the box.

> gardening   cancer   pizza   football   heart disease
> basketball   chips   education   salad   fish

Advertising of junk food such as (1)_____
and (2)_____ should be banned. Medical
problems, especially (3)_____ and some forms of
(4)_____ , are caused by bad diets. There are many
low-fat foods to choose from, like (5)_____ and
green (6)_____ . Team sports, for instance five-a-
side (7)_____ and (8)_____ , are
good social activities. One example of a cheap way to keep fit is
(9)_____ . Growing fruit and vegetables is good
exercise and puts food on the table. There are many ways to prevent
obesity. A case in point is (10)_____ . We must teach
children about the benefits of a balanced diet.

3 Complete the sentences below using the words and phrases in the
box together with your own ideas. The first has been done for you as
an example.

> such as   for instance   for example   especially

1 There are many ways to lose weight,
  <u>such as gardening and running</u>_____ .

2 Regular physical activity has a range of benefits,

  _____ .

3 Obesity can result in medical problems

  _____ .

4 Junk food can be found in many places,

  _____ .

5 Schools offer children the chance to do many sports,

  _____ .

6 There are a number of solutions to the problem of obesity

  _____ .

ACADEMIC WRITING SKILLS

WRITING SUPPORTING SENTENCES

1 Look at the words in bold in the paragraph below to see how the supporting sentences give reasons and examples.

Topic sentence	Eating a **balanced diet** is a great way for individuals to stay healthy, but **too much fat** in your diet can be a problem.
Supporting sentence 1: reason	A **balance of vitamins and minerals** helps your body maintain health.
Supporting sentence 2: examples	For example, we need **protein** from meat and **carbohydrates** from rice and bread, as well as **vitamins** from fruit and vegetables, in order to stay healthy.
Supporting sentence 3: reason	However, consuming **too much sugar and fat** in junk food such as fried chicken or cola drinks causes health risks.
Supporting sentence 4: examples	Obesity can lead to **heart disease** and **diabetes**.

2 Now write your own sentences in the table below to support the topic sentence about keeping fit.

Topic sentence	*Keeping fit is a great way for individuals to stay healthy, and too little exercise can lead to problems later in life.*
Supporting sentence 1: reason	_____
Supporting sentence 2: examples	_____
Supporting sentence 3: reason	_____
Supporting sentence 4: examples	_____

WRITING TASK

UNLOCK ONLINE

> What can people do to live longer? What can a government do to increase the average life expectancy of its country's citizens?

1 Use the words and phrases in the box to plan your essay.

> obesity and poor fitness   governments and individuals
> diet   physical activity   life expectancy

Introduction	(1)_____ decrease life expectancy
	(2)_____ can work together to increase life expectancy
Main body 1	Changes by individuals to their (3)_____ and their (4)_____ can increase life expectancy
Main body 2	Government initiatives to change their citizens' eating habits and exercise habits
Conclusion	Governments and individuals can work together to improve diet and fitness so that we can improve (5)_____

2 Write an essay to answer the Writing task. Use the plan above to help you. Remember to include an introduction, a main body paragraph giving individual solutions, another main body paragraph giving government solutions, and a conclusion.

3 Use the task checklist to review your essay for content and structure.

TASK CHECKLIST	✔
Have you followed the essay plan and included government and individual solutions?	
Have you used supporting sentences in each paragraph to give reasons and examples?	
Is there a conclusion which summarizes your essay and refers back to the essay topic in the introduction?	

4 Make any necessary changes to your essay.

5 Now use the language checklist to edit your essay for language errors which are common to B1 learners.

<table>
<tr><td>LANGUAGE CHECKLIST</td><td>✔</td></tr>
<tr><td>Have you used a range of academic verbs?</td><td></td></tr>
<tr><td>Have you used such as, like, for instance, especially and for example correctly to give examples?</td><td></td></tr>
<tr><td>Have you used to, in order to, so and so that correctly to give reasons?</td><td></td></tr>
</table>

6 Make any necessary changes to your essay.

OBJECTIVES REVIEW

7 Check your objectives.

I can ...

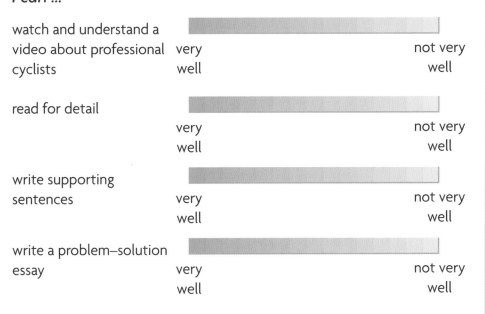

watch and understand a video about professional cyclists

very well   not very well

read for detail

very well   not very well

write supporting sentences

very well   not very well

write a problem–solution essay

very well   not very well

WORDLIST

UNIT VOCABULARY	ACADEMIC VOCABULARY	
balanced diet (n)	education (n)	involve (v)
calorie (n)	encourage (v)	provide (v)
heart disease (n)	evidence (n)	realize (v)
junk food (n)	exercise (n)	reduce (v)
life expectancy (n)	government (n)	solve (v)
obesity (n)	individual (n)	suffer (v)
self-esteem (n)	injure (v)	

LEARNING OBJECTIVES

Watch and listen	Watch and understand a video about the ASIMO robot
Reading skills	Scan to predict content
Academic writing skills	Edit for common errors
Writing task	Write an advantage–disadvantage essay

UNLOCK YOUR KNOWLEDGE

Work with a partner. Discuss the question below.

1 What do you think will happen in the world of science and technology in the next ten years?

2 Match the new technologies (1–3) to the definitions (a–c).

1	robotics	**a** the study of biology in order to copy nature and solve human problems
2	3D printing	**b** making plastic objects by printing designs on a computer
3	biomimicry	**c** the science of making and using robots

WATCH AND LISTEN

   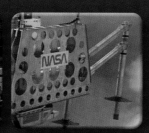  

PREPARING TO WATCH

USING VISUALS TO PREDICT CONTENT

1 You are going to watch a video about a special robot. Before you watch, look at the photographs of the robot and answer the questions below.

　1 What jobs are robots used for now?
　2 Can you think of any jobs robots might be used for in the future?

UNDERSTANDING
KEY VOCABULARY

2 Use the words and phrases in the box to complete the sentences below.

> mobility aid　gesture　centre of gravity
> uneven　disability　humanoid

　1 Something that looks like a human is _____ .
　2 An _____ surface is not flat.
　3 The point in an object where its weight is balanced is its
　　_____ .
　4 Something that helps you move is a _____ .
　5 A serious and long-term physical or mental problem that has a negative effect on your daily life is a _____ .
　6 A _____ is a movement of your hands, arms or head to express an idea or feeling.

WHILE WATCHING

UNDERSTANDING
MAIN IDEAS

3 ▶ Watch the video and number the main ideas (a–e) in the order that you hear them.

　a Uses for ASIMO _____
　b What similar robots will be able to do in the future _____
　c Background and history of ASIMO _____
　d What robots can do now _____
　e Recent improvements to ASIMO _____

4 The list below shows some of the things that ASIMO can do now and some things that robots like ASIMO will be able to do in the future. Tick (✔) the ones that ASIMO can do now.

1 play football   _____
2 balance on one foot   _____
3 jump   _____
4 walk on uneven surfaces _____
5 make tea   _____
6 push a cart   _____
7 open and close doors   _____
8 shake hands   _____
9 run down stairs   _____
10 speak English   _____
11 open a bottle   _____

5 ▶ Watch again and complete the sentences with a word or a number.

1 In 1986 the Honda automotive company wanted to create a humanoid _____ .

2 It took years to make ASIMO _____ on uneven surfaces.

3 ASIMO can run at _____ kph.

4 ASIMO is _____ cm tall.

5 ASIMO can hold _____ kg.

6 Researchers are working on robots that can respond to touch and _____ .

6 Work with a partner. Try to answer the questions below.

1 Why do you think that ASIMO was designed to have a humanoid shape?

2 Why was ASIMO designed to be smaller than a human, rather than the same size or taller?

3 What are the 'descendants of this robot' which are mentioned in the video?

DISCUSSION

7 Work with a partner. Discuss the questions below.

1 What are the advantages and disadvantages of using robots to do our housework for us?

2 What are the three most important inventions in the home? Why?

3 Which three inventions would you like to see in your home in the future?

READING 1

PREPARING TO READ

USING YOUR
KNOWLEDGE TO
PREDICT CONTENT

1 Answer the questions.

1 *bio* is a prefix which means 'life'. What words do you know that start
with *bio*?

2 Read the first paragraph of the article on page 127 opposite. What do
mimicry and *biomimicry* mean?

3 Can you think of any man-made objects that copy from something
in nature?

WHILE READING

SKIMMING

**UNLOCK
ONLINE**

2 Read the magazine article on page 127 opposite and answer the questions
below.

1 Which products are mentioned in the article?

2 Which plants or animals were copied to produce these products?

READING
FOR DETAIL

3 Read the article again and answer the questions below.

1 Where was George de Mestral from?

2 Which two features does Velcro® have, that allow it to stick together?

3 What does the shark's skin allow a shark to do?

4 What does the shark's skin do to bacteria?

5 Whose eyes did NASA want to protect from dangerous radiation?

6 What special feature of eagle eyes was copied to make sunglasses?

7 Which two features of a boxfish skeleton make it good for engineers
to copy?

8 What does the car copy, that allows it to save fuel?

READING BETWEEN THE LINES

MAKING
INFERENCES
FROM THE TEXT

4 Work with a partner. Answer the questions below.

1 Why do you think Velcro® became popular with children's
clothing companies?

2 Why do you think the Speedo Fastskin® swimsuit was controversial
during the Beijing Olympics?

3 Why do people have different opinions about the Bionic Car?

DISCUSSION

5 Work with a partner. Discuss the questions below.

1 Do you think biomimicry will be more common in the future? Why / Why not?

2 What are the advantages of copying from nature?

THE MAGIC OF MIMICRY

To mimic someone means to copy them. However, in science, people copy ideas from nature or natural processes to solve problems or to create products which will serve a specific purpose to help us. This is called biomimicry and its influence can be seen in many everyday products.

Perhaps the best-known example of biomimicry is Velcro®. It was invented in 1941 by a Swiss engineer called George de Mestral, who looked at the burdock seeds which stuck to his dog's hair. Under the microscope, he discovered that these seeds had hooks on them, so they stuck to loops on clothing or hair. He copied this idea and used strips of material with tiny hooks on them and strips of material with loose loops on. When he put both strips together they stuck like glue. However unlike glue, he could peel both strips apart and reattach them. Velcro® was initially unpopular with fashion companies but after it was used by NASA to stop items floating in space, it became popular with children's clothing companies.

More recently, swimwear has also been influenced by nature. The Speedo Fastskin®, a controversial swimsuit, was seen at the Beijing Olympics and worn by 28 of the 33 gold medal winners. The technology is based on the rough patterns on a shark's skin, which allows the shark to swim faster. Shark skin also stops bacteria growing on it, so scientists are copying this surface to design cleaner hospitals.

For NASA, protecting astronauts' eyes from the sun's rays is very important but protecting their eyes from other dangerous radiation is also essential. Scientists studied how eagles and falcons clearly recognize their prey. They discovered that they have yellow oil in their eyes which filters out harmful radiation and allows them to see very clearly. NASA copied this oil and it is now used by astronauts and pilots in Eagle Eyes® glasses. In addition to protecting eyes from all the dangerous rays, these sunglasses also improve vision in different weather conditions such as fog, sunlight or just normal light.

In another development, Mercedes-Benz has developed a new car which is based on the shape of the tropical boxfish. Engineers at Mercedes-Benz chose to copy the boxfish skeleton to make their Bionic Car because of its strength and low weight. The boxfish's bony body protects the animal's insides from injury in the same way as a car needs to protect the people inside it. The car's looks divide opinion but they are designed on the smooth shape of the boxfish. This shape also means the car has less air resistance and so uses less fuel.

It appears that the influence of biomimicry is unlimited, so it will be interesting to see what solutions nature provides us with in the future.

PREPARING TO READ

Scanning to predict content

When we scan a text, we do not read every word. We let our eyes move over the text, looking for key words that help us to understand what the text is about, before we read it carefully. For example, we can look for names, numbers, pronouns (*he, she, it, which, them, our*, etc.) or lists of words (e.g. words related to speed). This information helps us to think about what we expect the text to tell us.

SCANNING TO PREDICT CONTENT

1 You are going to read an article about technology in the future. Scan the article on page 129 opposite and answer the questions. Look out for the key words, which are in bold in the questions (1–3) below.

   1 Which paragraph (A–E) describes a **robot suit**?   _____

   2 Which paragraph (A–E) describes a **flying car**?   _____

   3 Which paragraph (A–E) describes a **3D printer**?   _____

WHILE READING

SKIMMING

UNLOCK ONLINE

2 Read the article and match the inventions (1–3) to their advantages (a–c) and their disadvantages (i–iii).

   1 flying cars

   2 3D printing

   3 a robot suit

   a **It** could **help** people walk again.

   b We could **avoid** speeding tickets.

   c We could **make** our own plastic products.

   i **Mechanical failure** might be a big problem.

   ii The main disadvantage is **cost**.

   iii The process is **slow and expensive**.

READING FOR DETAIL

3 Read the article again and write true (T), false (F) or does not say (DNS) next to the statements below.

   1 Flying cars will allow us to avoid traffic congestion on the roads. _____

   2 Mechanical failure will not be much of a problem for flying cars. _____

   3 We might be able to print things like necklaces or chairs in the future. _____

   4 3D printing was invented in 1984. _____

   5 BMW and Volkswagen are going to use 3D printing soon. _____

   6 Robot suits are heavy objects. _____

   7 The battery life of a robot suit is short at the moment. _____

The world of tomorrow

A What will the world of the future be like? There are plenty of people who are happy to give their opinion of what we will be doing in 2050. Here are three predictions about the world of tomorrow.

B When people talk about the future, we like to think that we will be able to drive out of our garages and take to the skies in our own personal flying car. The advantages are obvious. Some people predict this technology will allow complete three-dimensional freedom of movement. We could fly at 480 kilometres per hour, avoiding traffic lights, busy roads and speeding tickets. However, some people point to the disadvantages of flying cars. They claim that there are certain to be problems with traffic control. Another big problem is mechanical failure. What will happen if they break down? Also, if they become popular, there is likely to be another big problem: air traffic congestion. So it looks like flying cars face more then a few problems if they are to get off the ground!

C Most of us have printed out an electronic document on paper, but think about the possibility of printing out a three-dimensional object in plastic. 3D printers build an object using layers of liquid plastic. They build up the layers line-by-line like a normal printer until the object is complete. Vehicle companies like BMW and Volkswagen already use 3D printers to make life-size models of car parts. At the moment the process is slow and quality is low, but before long it might be possible to see a product on a website and then download it to your printer at home. In the future we could make our own furniture, jewellery, cups, plates, shoes and toys from designs on our computers, and reduce the amount of shopping we have to do.

D Imagine having your own Ironman suit. There are several companies trying to build a practical robot 'exoskeleton'. This is a suit of robot arms and legs which follows your movements. It will allow the wearer to lift heavy objects, walk long distances and even punch through walls! There are obvious military advantages for this technology but there are also benefits for people with disabilities. This suit might help people to walk again after disease or injury. However, the obvious disadvantage at the moment is cost. Even a simple exoskeleton can cost hundreds of thousands of pounds. Another problem is battery life. A suit like this needs a lot of power and so batteries only last about 15 minutes at the moment. One other problem is that a badly programmed robot suit could injure the wearer. You wouldn't want your robot leg or arm bending the wrong way.

E So in the future, although we might be able to fly to work, print out a pair of new shoes and lift a car above our heads, there are plenty of problems to solve before this will be possible.

READING BETWEEN THE LINES

MAKING
INFERENCES
FROM THE TEXT

4 Work with a partner. Answer the questions below.

1 Why is mechanical failure a problem in a flying car?
2 Why will flying cars cause more traffic congestion, not less?
3 What do you think could be the benefits of robot suits?
4 Why wouldn't you want a robot suit arm to bend the wrong way?

DISCUSSION

5 Work in pairs and answer the questions.

1 Do you think these inventions are a good idea? Why / Why not?
2 Choose one of the inventions. What would you do if you owned it?

⊙ LANGUAGE DEVELOPMENT

EXPLANATION

Making predictions

We use *will*, *could* and *won't* with an adverb before the main verb to talk about certainty in the future.

90% = *will definitely*

Cars **will definitely** become more efficient in the future.

70% = *will probably*

The next generation **will probably** use more digital devices.

50% = *could possibly*

We **could possibly** see humans walking on Mars soon.

30% = *probably won't*

We **probably won't** have flying cars.

10% = *definitely won't*

We **definitely won't** be travelling to other stars.

1 Complete the sentences about the future using the verb and adverb phrases in the box on page 130.

1 In years to come, biofuels _____ become more important.

2 Genetic modification _____ be very controversial before the decade is out.

3 In the near future, electronic human implants _____ become commonplace.

4 Biomimicry _____ be a growth industry before too long.

5 Robotic cars _____ be everyday products within the next ten years.

2 Look again at Exercise 1 and underline the phrases that refer to future time.

Understanding prefixes

We add prefixes to the beginning of a word to make a new word with a different meaning. Understanding the meaning of prefixes can help you guess the general meaning of difficult academic or technical words.

3 Look at these prefixes and their meanings. Use words with these prefixes to make five predictions about new technology.

prefix	meaning	example
auto-	self	automatic
de-	reverse	demotivate
dis-	reverse or remove	disagree
mis-	badly	misuse
post-	after	post-modern
pre-	before	prehistoric
re-	again	rewrite
sub-	under	submerge
un-	remove, reverse, not	unpack
under-	less than	undercook

4 Compare the pairs of sentences below. Use the table and say whether the sentences have the same or opposite meanings.

1 Flying cars are **unsafe**.
   Flying cars are dangerous.

2 The discovery was made by **postgraduate** students.
   The discovery was made by students who haven't graduated from university yet.

3 The robots **underperformed** in their tests.
   The robots performed better than we expected in their tests.

4 We have to **rethink** the way we use technology.
   We have to think again about how we use technology.

5 Genetic engineering **dehumanizes** us.
   Genetic engineering makes us less human.

6 People often **misunderstand** new inventions.
   People often understand new inventions perfectly.

7 The car flies on **autopilot**.
   The car flies without a human pilot.

8 The chip is inserted in a **subcutaneous** layer of the skin.
   The chip is put under the skin.

CRITICAL THINKING

At the end of this unit, you will write an advantage–disadvantage essay. Look at the Writing task in the box below.

> Choose one new area of technology or invention and outline its advantages and disadvantages.

Listing

Making a list is an important skill which will help you to organize your ideas for your writing. You can brainstorm the ideas alone or in a group.

REMEMBER

1 Are the words and phrases in the box advantages or disadvantages of the inventions in Reading 2? Complete the table on page 133.

> mechanical failure   super strong   low quality   possible injury
> freedom of movement   help people with disability
> very expensive   traffic control problems   do less shopping
> slow   avoid traffic congestion   make your own products

	advantages	disadvantages
flying cars	• _____ _____ • _____ _____	• _____ _____ • _____ _____
3D printing	• _____ _____ • _____ _____	• _____ _____ • _____ _____
robot suits	• _____ _____ • _____ _____	• _____ _____ • _____ _____

Reasoning

When we think critically, we have to find reasons for what we read or write about. This involves thinking of your own ideas and then finding evidence to support those ideas.

2 Work in groups of four. Write about your predictions for two inventions (1–2). Say what the advantages and disadvantages are. Some predictions have been done for you as examples.

1 Food: Genetic modification	Advantages: Larger types of rice, wheat and vegetables could be grown Food could be grown with less water in hot countries Disadvantages: Modified seeds would be expensive Possible health problems in the future
2 Education: Computer schoolbooks	Advantages: Disadvantages:
3 _____ _____	Advantages: Disadvantages:

3 Now think of an invention and complete the third row of the table.

WRITING

GRAMMAR FOR WRITING

EXPLANATION

Relative clauses

We use relative clauses to give more information about something without starting a new sentence. We use *who* after people and *which* after things. Notice that we also avoid repeating the object of the sentence this way.

> Velcro® was invented in 1941 by George de Mestral. **George de Mestral saw the seeds on his dog's hair.**
>
> Velcro® was invented in 1941 by George de Mestral, **who saw the seeds on his dog's hair.**

1 Join each pair of sentences to make one sentence, using a relative clause. Take out the repeated words.

1 Scientists are developing new robots.
New robots will be able to do dangerous work.

_____

2 There is a great deal of research to help elderly people.
Elderly people will benefit from this new technology.

_____

3 There is a lot of new investment in biofuels.
Biofuels are cleaner and more sustainable than fossil fuels.

_____

4 This technology will save energy.
Saving energy is good for the environment.

_____

5 The concept car has a special design.
A special design makes the concept car more fuel efficient.

_____

6 The research will be done by scientists at the University of Cambridge.
Scientists at the University of Cambridge hope to publish the research next year.

_____

2 In questions 5 and 6, which repeated words can be replaced with *it*?

Advantages and disadvantages

To make an essay clearer for the reader, we can use prepositional phrases to introduce the advantages and disadvantages of a subject at the start of a new sentence.

3 Complete the table below with the phrases (1–8).

1 The main **advantage/disadvantage of** ... is ...
2 The main **worry about** ... is ...
3 One **point against** ... is ...
4 One **good/bad thing about** ... is ...
5 Perhaps the biggest **concern with** ... is
6 A real **benefit of** ... is ...
7 The main argument **in favour of / against** ... is ...
8 The **problem with** ... is ...

A positive arguments	B negative arguments

4 Choose a negative or positive phrase from Exercise 3 to complete the sentences below. More than one answer is possible.

1 _____ about robots is that they can do dangerous or boring jobs instead of humans.

2 _____ against genetic engineering is that it may cause pollution.

3 _____ of medical imaging is that you can see clearly inside patients' bodies.

4 _____ with robots is that they take jobs away from people.

5 _____ about flying cars is that they could crash, causing terrible accidents.

ACADEMIC WRITING SKILLS

Common errors

When you are writing it can be easy to miss out small words. This can be a problem for the reader, especially if there are too many mistakes in one paragraph. The reader may lose confidence in your ideas as well as your English.

1 Read the paragraph below and write one word in each gap.

Computer schoolbooks are expected (1)_____ become very important in the near future for a number (2)_____ reasons. Before the end of (3)_____ decade, students will probably all have tablet computers, which will carry all of the books they need, (4)_____ well as offer access (5)_____ the internet. However, there could (6)_____ some disadvantages to using computer schoolbooks (7)_____ the future. One problem (8)_____ that they could possibly get broken in school bags. These tablet computers will also be expensive (9)_____ buy and replace, which (10)_____ probably mean less money for teachers. Overall, computer schoolbooks seem (11)_____ a good idea but they are unlikely to be successful unless they (12)_____ tough and cheap.

2 Correct the common spelling mistakes in the sentences below.

1 Many major universities are studing artificial intelligence.

2 Scientists have tryed to make this technology work.

3 Inventions cost a lot of mony.

4 It is ture that flying cars are dangerous.

5 It is realy important to use new technology.

6 Robots are machines wich can move on their own.

7 There are many diffrent scientific discoveries every year.

8 Peaple are sometimes afraid of new technology.

9 It will be expensive to equip schools withe tablet computers.

10 Inventors belive the future will be improved by new technology.

WRITING TASK

Choose one new area of technology or invention and outline its advantages and disadvantages.

1 Use your notes from the Critical thinking section on page 132 to answer the task. Remember to include an introduction with references to two or three new areas of discovery or invention. You should then have two or three main body paragraphs with advantages and disadvantages, and a conclusion.

2 Use the task checklist to review your essay for content and structure.

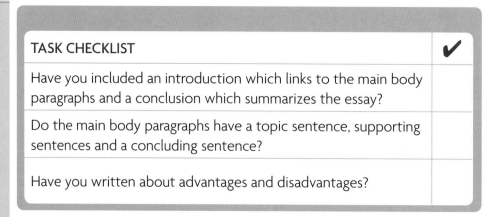

TASK CHECKLIST	✔
Have you included an introduction which links to the main body paragraphs and a conclusion which summarizes the essay?	
Do the main body paragraphs have a topic sentence, supporting sentences and a concluding sentence?	
Have you written about advantages and disadvantages?	

3 Make any necessary changes to your essay.

4 Now use the language checklist to edit your essay for language errors which are common to B1 learners.

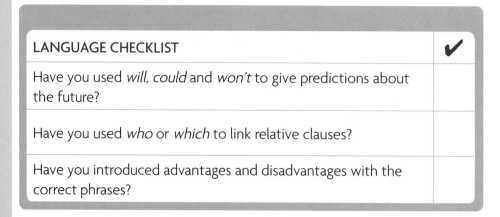

LANGUAGE CHECKLIST	✔
Have you used *will*, *could* and *won't* to give predictions about the future?	
Have you used *who* or *which* to link relative clauses?	
Have you introduced advantages and disadvantages with the correct phrases?	

5 Make any necessary changes to your essay.

OBJECTIVES REVIEW

6 Check your objectives.

I can ...

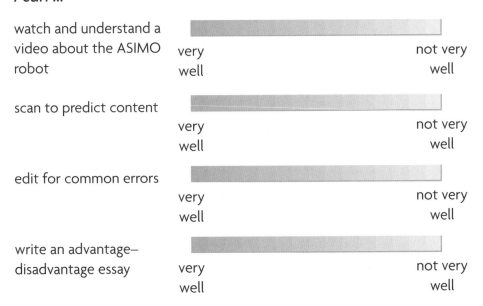

watch and understand a video about the ASIMO robot

very well   not very well

scan to predict content

very well   not very well

edit for common errors

very well   not very well

write an advantage–disadvantage essay

very well   not very well

WORDLIST

UNIT VOCABULARY	ACADEMIC VOCABULARY
biofuel (n)	advantage (n)
centre of gravity (n)	benefit (n)
disability (n)	concern (n)
genetic modification (n)	definitely (adv)
gesture (n)	disadvantage (n)
	discovery (n)
	innovation (n)
	possibly (adv)
	probably (adv)
	scientific (adj)

LEARNING OBJECTIVES

Watch and listen	Watch and understand a video about the Missoni fashion house
Reading skills	Distinguish fact from opinion
Academic writing skills	Edit for cohesion and coherence
Writing task	Write a balanced opinion essay

UNL⌀CK YOUR KNOWLEDGE

Work with a partner. Discuss the questions below.

1 Which clothing brands are popular in your country?

2 Why do people buy branded clothing?

3 Do you prefer branded clothing or clothes that do not have a brand name?

4 Are shops that sell cheap clothes popular in your country?

WATCH AND LISTEN

PREPARING TO WATCH

USING VISUALS TO PREDICT CONTENT

1 Look at the photographs above and answer the questions below.

   1 What can you see in the photographs?

   2 What industry is shown?

2 Match the words and phrases (1–5) to the definitions (a–e).

   1 fashion capital

   2 collection

   3 label

   4 Fashion Week

   5 critic

   a a manufacturer of clothing which can be recognized by its design and logo

   b a person who reviews or comments on what they see

   c a city in which fashion is the dominant or central activity

   d clothing for a new season

   e a show in which new collections are presented to the public for the first time

WHILE WATCHING

UNDERSTANDING MAIN IDEAS

3 ▶ Watch the video and choose the best description of the topic.

   a New York Fashion Week

   b The city of Milan

   c Changes in fashion

   d A family business

4 ▶ Watch again and circle the correct words to complete the statements below.

1 Milan is Italy's *second / third* biggest city.
2 Angela's *brothers / parents* started the Missoni label.
3 Angela runs Missoni with her *sisters / brothers*.
4 *400 / 800* people work in Missoni's factory.
5 Angela has to choose *suits / dresses* to include in the show.

5 Complete the sentences below using the information in the box. Then watch again and check your answers.

| one-bedroom | twice a year | $250 million | $6 billion | 800 | 1953 |

1 The Missoni factory employs _____ people.
2 The Missoni label was started in _____ .
3 Each year the fashion industry makes _____ .
4 Missoni makes _____ a year.
5 Fashion Week takes place _____ in Milan.
6 The Missoni label began life in a _____ flat.

DISCUSSION

6 Work with a partner. Discuss the questions below.

1 What kind of clothes are you most comfortable in? Describe your favourite outfit.
2 Are you interested in fashion? Do you own anything with a designer label?
3 Do you think that young people are too interested in their appearance?

READING 1

PREPARING TO READ

USING YOUR KNOWLEDGE TO PREDICT CONTENT

1 Answer the questions below.

1 Does fast fashion imply cheap or expensive clothes?
2 How many times a year do fashions usually change?
3 What would happen if fashion designers changed fashions every month?

2 Now read the web article on page 145 opposite and check your answers.

WHILE READING

READING FOR MAIN IDEAS

UNL⊙CK
ONLINE

3 Read the article again and number the main ideas (a–f) in the order that they are mentioned. Not all the ideas are mentioned.

a designer clothing   _____
b advantages of fast fashion   _____
c Fast fashion shows   _____
d the definition of fast fashion _____
e advertising fast fashion   _____
f disadvantages of fast fashion _____

READING FOR DETAIL

4 Look at the article again and correct the factual mistakes in the sentences below. The first one has been done for you as an example.

1 Traditional fashion retailers annually produce ~~10,000~~ 2,000 items.

2 Fast-fashion designs that are unpopular are withdrawn in less than a month.

3 Traditional fashion is good for the customer because of the greater volume of sales.

4 The biggest problem with fast fashion is the theft of ideas.

5 Cotton growers need to produce more so they have to use more water.

6 Designer clothing is taking off in the West.

7 Designer clothes are good for the economy because they last a long time.

Is *fast fashion* taking over?

It is estimated that the high-street fashion industry is worth around £45bn in the UK alone. Traditionally, fashion retailers had four collections per year, one for each season, but nowadays fast-fashion companies can design and manufacture clothes in as little as four weeks. Fast fashion means that the latest designs that appear at the fashion shows in Paris, London and Milan can be copied and in high-street shops within a month. This means a typical fast-fashion retailer can stock 10,000 items annually, compared with 2,000 for its competitors.

The advantages of rapidly changing fashions are clear. Shortening the product life cycle means if a design doesn't sell well within a week, it is taken out of the shops and a new design is chosen. This is good for the manufacturer as it means greater volumes of sales, and good for the customer as they can keep up with fast-moving trends cheaply – and every time they visit the store, there is something new.

However, there are also a number of disadvantages to this approach. Perhaps the biggest concern is the impact on the environment of wasted clothes. Buying twelve new sets of clothes rather than four means that more textiles will be thrown away. Furthermore, with fashions changing so quickly, cotton growers need to produce more cotton more cheaply, and that means using more pesticides and chemicals.

The other problem is the theft of ideas. Fashion houses invest a lot of time and money on new ideas, only to see these ideas copied for free by fast-fashion companies.

At the other end of the scale in the fashion industry is high-end designer clothing. At the same time as fast fashion is taking off in the West, Asian consumers are buying more and more expensive, luxury brands. Many buy branded clothes just to show that they can afford them but others choose them for quality, saying that they will last longer. They may have a point. Expensive designer clothes will last and therefore be more environmentally friendly because of their long lifespan.

It seems that the fashion industry is changing almost as fast as the fashion it produces – but what do you think? We'd like to hear your comments about the fashion industry today.

Comments
6 comments

Carmen Reply
I'd love to have the money to buy designer clothes but I have to buy cheaper products because I don't have much money. I'm sure the quality is not as good as with designer labels.

 Like 14

Ahmet Reply

Designer fashion is a waste of money. Wearing brand names is just free advertising for that company and I don't think the quality is any different.

 Like 13

Jasmine Reply

Great article!

I love fast fashion! I enjoy looking good and having lots of clothes. Fast fashion allows me to buy lots of clothes really cheaply. Why should I feel bad about throwing cheap clothes in the bin when they go out of fashion? I can just go out and get more.

 Like 0

Ben Reply

Response to Jasmine

People like you make me really angry. That is such a selfish attitude. Think about the environment. Don't you care about wasting all that cotton? At least give the clothes to charity shops if you don't want them anymore.

 Like 7

Sara Reply

Style is important to me. I study fashion at university and I would never buy fast fashion. I don't want to look like everyone else. I prefer to buy second-hand clothes because older clothes were designed to last. I have my own style. I don't need to copy Paris or Milan.

Like 11

Fatima Reply

I can understand why people like fast fashion but I prefer to pay for quality, and if the store has ethically produced clothes then that is perfect. I agree with Ben: we need to look after the planet, otherwise our children won't have a planet to live on. I would rather pay more and know I'm doing good. It's time more people got a conscience!

 Like 31

READING BETWEEN THE LINES

MAKING
INFERENCES
FROM THE TEXT

5 Look at the comments about the article and answer the questions below.

1 Who is against designer fashion? _____
2 Who wants to buy more expensive clothes? _____
3 Who doesn't like to follow fashion trends? _____
4 Who has the most likes? Why? _____
5 Who has the fewest likes? Why? _____

DISCUSSION

6 Work with a partner. Discuss the questions below.

1 Do you have any fast-fashion shops in your country? If so, which ones?
2 Do you like the idea of fast fashion?
3 Is fashion more important to younger or older people? Why?

UNL○CK READING AND WRITING SKILLS 3

READING 2

PREPARING TO READ

1 Work with a partner. Try to answer the questions below.

USING YOUR
KNOWLEDGE TO
PREDICT CONTENT

1 Why do companies move their factories to other countries?
2 What are the benefits for a country when a multinational company locates its production there?
3 Are there any disadvantages for workers in the country where the company is based when companies manufacture their products in different countries?

2 Now read the newspaper article below and check your answers.

OFFSHORE PRODUCTION

A The world's consumption of fashion is huge. The European Union imported textiles (clothing and carpets) to the value of €83.7 billion in 2010*. Prices have fallen, too, with hand-finished shirts costing less than five euros. To make clothes at these low prices, companies have to keep costs down. They use offshore production to do this. Large companies make their products in developing countries where workers are paid much less than in developed countries.

B Multinational companies are careful of their reputation for fairness, so they try hard to make sure local pay and conditions are legal. Supporters of overseas production facilities argue that most multinationals pay the correct minimum wage in the country and sometimes pay more. However, factory workers may actually only earn a few cents to make an item which would sell for hundreds of dollars. This low pay means low labour costs, and the multinational company keeps most of the profit.

C Multinational companies argue that they meet local employment laws and claim that they refuse to work with factories which do not follow their rules. Critics, however, call these kinds of factories 'sweatshops'. They argue that employees are made to do long hours of work, often in dangerous conditions, and do not get paid overtime.

D Overseas manufacturing plants have been in the media because they sometimes employ children. Supporters argue that often school is too expensive for some children and that children who work in factories are protected from worse jobs on the streets or in the fields. However, critics of overseas production state that child labour is wrong. They claim that children should be in full-time education rather than working in a factory.

E Another point that should be considered is that developing countries encourage developed countries to invest in them to provide jobs. Supporters of overseas production point out that increased investment has positive effects in the long term. Nobel prize-winning economist Paul Krugman points out that the growth in manufacturing has an impact on the rest of the economy, because it reduces the number of people needing to work in agriculture and increases competition for labour. This leads to higher wages, which lead to other improvements, such as the ability to send children to school. On the other hand, the disadvantage of this foreign investment is the fact that it can have a negative impact on the economy of developed countries, because people lose their jobs when production is outsourced to other countries.

F It seems that if multinationals are going to benefit from low production costs by using overseas suppliers, they should do more to improve the social situation – for example, by building schools for the children in those communities. It is also clear that multinationals should invest in communities in the developed countries where they sell their products. In conclusion, there are clear benefits for the multinationals in terms of the lower costs of production in developing countries and their workers, but they should still do more to protect the workers in overseas manufacturing plants.

*European Commission 2011

3 Match the words and phrases (1–8) to their definitions (a–h).

1 offshore production
2 multinational company
3 low pay
4 employee
5 pay and conditions
6 labour costs
7 consumption
8 manufacturing plant

a the amount of a product that is bought and used
b wages that are below the usual level
c the amount a company spends on employing workers
d factory
e a large business which operates in many countries
f wages, salaries and working arrangements
g making products in factories that are in other countries
h worker

WHILE READING

4 Read the article again and match the ideas in the box to the paragraphs (A–E). The first one has been done for you as an example.

> minimum wage   dangerous conditions   education   local laws
> child labour   increased investment   low-cost textiles
> huge import volume   lost jobs   low pay

A	low-cost textiles, huge import volume
B	_____
C	_____
D	_____
E	_____

5 Complete the sentences using a word from the article for each gap.

1 A _____ is a name for a factory where a lot of people work long hours for not very much money.
2 Many famous fashion companies have been in the _____ because their working conditions were poor.
3 People argue that sweatshop workers are paid badly; however, multinationals often pay more than the _____ wage.
4 Critics claim that multinationals do not follow local _____ laws.

READING BETWEEN THE LINES

Distinguishing fact from opinion

When we read a text, we need to be able to decide which points are facts and which points are opinions.

6 Complete the table below by deciding whether the points (1–6) are facts, the author's opinion or opinions of other people.

	fact	author opinion	other opinion
1 'The European Union imported textiles ... to the value of €86.7 billion in 2010.'			
2 'Supporters of overseas production facilities argue that most multinationals pay the correct minimum wage ...'			
3 'Multinational companies argue that they meet local employment laws ...'			
4 'Critics of overseas production ... claim that children should be in full-time education ...'			
5 'It seems that ... multinationals ... should do more to improve the social situation ...'			
6 'It is also clear that multinationals should invest in communities in ... developed countries'			

DISCUSSION

7 Work with a partner. Discuss the questions below.

1 Do you think overseas production of clothing is a good idea?
2 Do you think that multinationals that invest in developing countries should do more for the local community? Why / Why not?

Hyponyms

A hyponym is a more specific word for something that can also be described using a more general word. For example, *crimson* and *scarlet* are types of the colour *red*, and so the words *crimson* and *scarlet* are hyponyms of the word *red*. In the same way, *red* is a hyponym of *colour*.

UNLOCK
ONLINE

1 Add the hyponyms in the box to the chart below. Use the Glossary on page 197 to check the meaning of new words.

> wool   high-heeled shoes   T-shirt   beauty products
> natural fibres   nylon   jeans   casual clothes

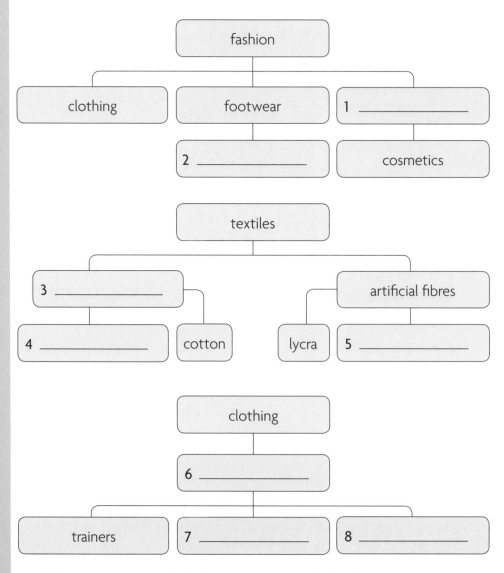

2 Add five more types of clothes to each part of the chart.

Homonyms

A homonym is a word that has same spelling and pronunciation as another word, but a different meaning. Many words in the Academic Wordlist are homonyms of more common words. Check you know which meaning is used by looking at the context of the word in the sentence.

3 Read the sentences (1–8) and decide whether the word in bold is being used with the general meaning (A) or the academic meaning (B) given in the table of homonyms below.

1 Trade restrictions have been **relaxed** in recent years resulting in more imports. _____
2 The **volume** of sales in luxury brands is increasing. _____
3 There was **drama** last night when it was revealed that a leading fashion manufacturer had been using children to produce clothes. _____
4 The **goal** of the community investment programme is to build new schools in the communities that the company works in. _____
5 The **brief** was to produce a range of clothes which are attractive to young sportspeople. _____
6 Multinationals have a tough **approach** to child labour and cancel their contracts with companies which employ children. _____
7 Multinationals work hard to **accommodate** the requirements of local governments. _____
8 This **area** of the plant is where the textiles are dyed and washed. _____

	A general meaning	B academic meaning
to relax	to become calmer	to make a rule less strict
volume	a sound level	an amount of something
drama	a play	excitement
goal	a point scored in a ball game	an aim
brief	short	instructions
approach	coming nearer	a method
to accommodate	to give someone a place to stay	to give someone what is needed
area	a piece of land	an academic subject

CRITICAL THINKING

At the end of this unit, you will write a balanced opinion essay. Look at this unit's Writing task in the box below.

> Fashion is harmful. Discuss.

Identifying arguments and counter-arguments

In an argumentative essay, we make points (arguments) which we then respond to (counter-arguments).

EVALUATE

1 Complete the table below with the arguments and counter-arguments (1–14). The first two have been done for you as examples.

A arguments in favour of fashion	B arguments against fashion
(1) creates new jobs	(2) causes too much waste

1 creates new jobs
2 causes too much waste
3 encourages child labour
4 bad pay for overseas workers
5 lets you show your personality
6 helps children make friends
7 is important to the economy
8 designer brands promote materialism
9 allows people to show their social group
10 pressures children to look like adults
11 makes children worry about their size
12 brings investment to developing countries
13 makes people look silly
14 keeps us warm and comfortable

WRITING

GRAMMAR FOR WRITING

Prepositional phrases
Prepositional phrases can be used to join two pieces of information.

1 Answer the questions (1–3) below about the meaning of the phrases in the box.

> apart from   rather than   in addition to
> instead of   except for   along with

1 Which two phrases mean *in preference to*?
2 Which two phrases mean *not including*?
3 Which two phrases mean *and*?

2 Complete the sentences using the phrases in the box above.

1 _____ buying disposable fashion, it is better for the environment to choose clothes that last longer.
2 The company closed its offshore production facilities _____ its overseas retail stores.
3 Most people prefer wearing casual clothes _____ formal business suits.
4 _____ perfume, I don't use any designer products.
5 _____ encouraging child labour, offshore production also drives wages and working conditions down.
6 You can't wear any jewellery in the factory _____ wedding rings.

Counter-arguments

Look at the tables and the example writing below, which show how to give other people's opinions.

Supporters Proponents		are in favour of	
	of X		Y.
Critics Opponents		are against	

They	argue claim insist state	that	X	is an important factor in plays a central role in plays an important part in has a positive/negative impact on	Y (because …).

Supporters of moving production overseas are in favour of foreign investment. They insist that this investment plays a central role in improving the economy in developing countries.

Critics of offshore production are against moving jobs abroad. They claim that this activity is an important factor in unemployment in developed countries.

3 Answer the questions using language from the examples in the box above.

1 What do the supporters and critics of fast fashion think about it?
2 What do the supporters and critics of designer labels think about them?
3 What do the supporters and critics of fashion magazines think about them?

ACADEMIC WRITING SKILLS

Cohesion

At B1 level, students often make mistakes by missing out important subjects, verbs and conjunctions when they are writing. This means the text loses its cohesion and it becomes difficult to follow because the parts that hold it together are missing.

1 Complete the paragraph using the words in the box.

> style   clothes   ones   they   fashion
> that   and   clothing   these   This

The speed of change in the fashion world means that we buy many more (1)_____ than we need and throw away unused (2)_____ just because (3)_____ are out of fashion. To keep up with the pace of (4)_____ , new shops have recently opened offering clothes made as cheaply as possible so we can throw clothes away ready to buy the next season's (5)_____ . (6)_____ way of buying clothes means that more cotton needs to be used and (7)_____ means more intensive agriculture (8)_____ damage to the environment. In addition, many of (9)_____ clothes are sewn in sweatshops in developing countries where children and women are paid less than a dollar a day for their work, while the (10)_____ companies in developed countries keep the profit.

Coherence

Even when we check our spelling on a computer, we can still make mistakes if the word is wrong. Using the wrong word can make the text lose coherence – that is, the reader cannot understand the meaning.

2 Find the mistakes in the sentences below and correct them.

1 Second-hand clothes are more environmentally friendly then fast fashion.
2 We buy more clothes, even thought we do not need them.
3 Spending too much on luxury brands is a bed idea.
4 Some designer products are just two expensive.
5 I thing people spend too much time on fashion.
6 Some people bye too many designer bags which they don't need.
7 It just isn't health to try and copy those thin fashion models.
8 Body image is quiet a big problem for some teenage girls.

WRITING TASK

PLAN

> Fashion is harmful. Discuss.

1 Think about the advantages and disadvantages of fashion. Use the outline below to plan your essay. Include your ideas from the Critical thinking section on page 152.

Introduction	• Introduce the topic. • Include a sentence about the main arguments. • Include a sentence about the main counter-arguments
Main body paragraphs	• Give argument 1 and counter-argument 1. • Give argument 2 and counter-argument 2. • Give argument 3 and counter-argument 3.
Conclusion	• Give a summary of main arguments. • Say if any of the arguments are particularly strong. • Say which arguments you agree with. • Give your own argument if you can think of a different one.

2 Answer the Writing task by writing an essay with four paragraphs, following your plan in Exercise 1.

WRITE A FIRST DRAFT

3 Use the task checklist to review your essay for content and structure.

EDIT

TASK CHECKLIST	✔
Is there an introduction, a main body and a conclusion?	
Have you discussed both the advantages and the disadvantages of fashion?	
Have you used counter-arguments to fully discuss the topic?	

4 Make any necessary changes to your essay.

5 Now use the language checklist to edit your essay for language errors which are common to B1 learners.

UNL**O**CK READING AND WRITING SKILLS 3

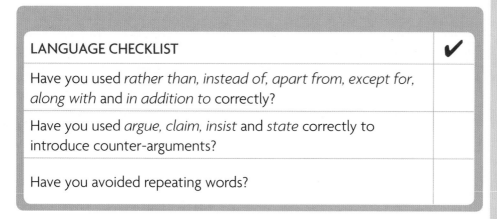

LANGUAGE CHECKLIST	✔
Have you used *rather than, instead of, apart from, except for, along with* and *in addition to* correctly?	
Have you used *argue, claim, insist* and *state* correctly to introduce counter-arguments?	
Have you avoided repeating words?	

6 Make any necessary changes to your essay.

OBJECTIVES REVIEW

7 Check your objectives.

I can ...

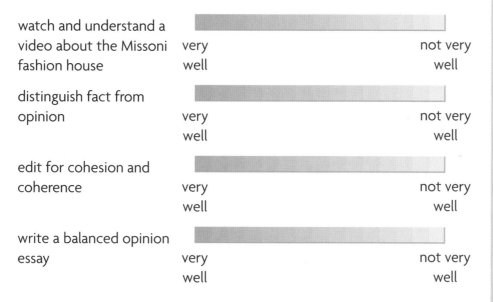

watch and understand a video about the Missoni fashion house

very well   not very well

distinguish fact from opinion

very well   not very well

edit for cohesion and coherence

very well   not very well

write a balanced opinion essay

very well   not very well

WORDLIST

UNIT VOCABULARY	ACADEMIC VOCABULARY
artificial fibres (n)	accommodate (v)
beauty products (n)	approach (n)
casual clothes (n)	area (n)
consumption (n)	brief (adj)
employee (n)	drama (n)
manufacturing plant (n)	goal (n)
multinational company (n)	relax (v)
natural fibres (n)	volume (n)
textile (n)	

LEARNING OBJECTIVES

Watch and listen	Watch and understand a video about an emerging economy
Reading skills	Skim a text
Academic writing skills	Write a description of a graph
Writing task	Write an explanatory paragraph describing a graph

UNL⌀CK YOUR KNOWLEDGE

Answer the questions about your country or region.

1 What kinds of agricultural crops are produced in your country?

2 What kinds of things are made in your country?

3 What kinds of services are there where you live?

4 How has the economy of your country changed in recent years?

WATCH AND LISTEN

PREPARING TO WATCH

USING YOUR
KNOWLEDGE TO
PREDICT CONTENT

1 Work with a partner. Try to answer the questions below.

   1 How do countries make money (e.g. tourism, taxation)?

   2 Which of the countries (a–d) do you think is the world's biggest exporter of oil?

     a Norway   **c** Venezuela

     b Saudi Arabia   **d** Russia

2 You are going to watch a video about Russia. Before you watch, try to answer the questions below.

   1 What is the weather like in Russia?

   2 Do you think there are a lot of rich people in Russia? Why? / Why not?

   3 Do you think Russia has a successful economy?

UNDERSTANDING
KEY VOCABULARY

3 Complete the gaps in the sentences using the collocations in the box below.

> standard of living   natural resources   economic stability
> retailing   investment bank   economic growth

   1 If the economy of a country doesn't change much, it has

     _____ .

   2 An _____ helps companies buy and sell shares, or helps them to buy other companies.

   3 The amount of money and comfort people have in a particular society is their _____ .

   4 Minerals, forests, coal, etc. which can be used by people are

     _____ .

   5 If a country's economy is increasing in size, the country is experiencing

     _____ .

   6 Selling goods to the public rather than to businesses is

     _____ .

WHILE WATCHING

4 ▶ Watch the video and number the main ideas (a–e) in the order that you hear them.

UNDERSTANDING
MAIN IDEAS

a Reasons why the economy is growing _____

b Economic problems after the end of the Soviet Union _____

c What will happen in the future _____

d How oil wealth has affected Russians _____

e How oil wealth has affected the Russian economy _____

5 ▶ Watch again and complete the lecture notes.

Past	Present	Future
Oil wealth created a lot of (1)_____	Russia has over one hundred (3)_____	The oil is (5)_____
These people invested in (2)_____	Retail sales are (4)_____	It is predicted that the oil will only last for another (8)_____

6 Work with a partner. Try to answer the questions below.

1 How did oil restart the economy and lift many Russians out of poverty?

2 Why do multinational companies want to invest in Russia?

DISCUSSION

7 Work with a partner. Discuss the questions below.

1 What are the dangers for a country of relying on one major source of income?

2 What does your country import and export?

3 How will the economy of your country change in the future?

PREPARING TO READ

1 Match the words and phrases (1–8) to their definitions (a–h).

1	recession	a an expensive mineral like gold, silver and platinum
2	stocks and shares	b putting money into something to make a profit
		c profit
3	investor	d parts of a publicly owned business which can be bought and sold
4	market value	
5	precious metal	e when the economy gets smaller
6	investment	f what people will generally pay for something
7	interest rate	g a person who puts money into something to make a profit
8	return on investment	
		h the percentage that a bank charges you when you borrow money, or what it pays you when you keep money in an account

2 Answer the questions.

1 If you want to make some money, what can you invest in?
2 Do you think it is better to invest in gold or in classic cars?

WHILE READING

3 Read the article on page 163 and see whether gold, classic cars or another investment is best.

4 Complete the summary using no more than two words from the article for each gap.

The article looks at the performance of two different ways of (1)_____ your money: gold, and (2)_____ . Although gold (3)_____ have risen considerably over the period discussed, the best way to make use of and (4)_____ your investment appears to be buying classic cars. From the cars shown on the graph, the Aston Martin DB5 saloon provides the biggest (5)_____ on investment at 3,000%. However, the best (6)_____ ever seems to be the James Bond car, which is now worth an unbelievable £1.5m. When investing in classic cars, you should remember that it is a (7)_____ business and changes in (8)_____ mean that choosing the right car is difficult.

How should you invest your money?

In a recession, interest rates are low. This means that investing your money in a bank may not be the best way of making money. So what might be the better options?

Stocks and shares are also risky when the economy takes a dive, so where should you invest to make the most of your money? For the brave investor, there are a range of alternative investments, such as precious metals, famous paintings and Ferraris. Gold bars and coins are a popular investment because it is easy to see how the market value changes over time.

Here we can see the sharp rise in gold prices over the last decade, from 2001 to 2011. For the first

three years, the price stayed the same, at about £200 per ounce. However, in the second half of 2005 there was a dramatic increase in the price of gold, to nearly £400. Over the next year, the price was stable and it stayed this way until late 2007. This was the beginning of the sharp upward trend, which has continued for the last four years. The price of gold peaked at just under £1,200 in late 2011. Gold prices are expected to rise to around £3,500 by the year 2020, so it looks like a good time to invest. However, it may be wise to take one famous investor's advice. Warren Buffet, one of the richest men in the world, dislikes gold as an investment. He points out that since 1965 the total return on gold was 4,455%. But the total return on stocks and shares was higher, at 6,072%. He also says it is better for society to use your money for something productive then have it sitting in a bank.

So stocks and shares are clearly the best option, but some people prefer to be able to use and enjoy their investment. Classic cars are proving to be one way to have fun and make lots of money. In fact, over the last

thirty years, the value of some classic cars has risen far more than both gold and house prices. A 1972 Ferrari Dino 246 cost £9,000 in 1980 but is worth £150,000 now. And a 1955 Mercedes Benz 300SL cost £25,000 in 1980 but is worth an amazing £500,000 now. But the classic car that provides the biggest return on investment is a 1964 Aston Martin DB5 saloon. This cost £10,000 in 1980 and is now worth £300,000. This is an increase of 3,000% – in other words, it cost half the price of an average UK house in 1980 but is worth almost twice as much as the average one now! However, none of these cars compare to what is perhaps the best investment ever: a man in Tennessee bought the DB5 that was used in two of the James Bond films. It cost just £5,000 in 1970 but it is now worth over one and a half million pounds! This is an incredible 20,000% increase!

One thing to remember with investment is that it is a risky business. Classic cars need to be kept in excellent condition to get the increase in value and, because fashions change, investors need to know which car to choose. Repairs are very expensive and you need to know which car will increase most in value. You may make a big profit but there is no guarantee.

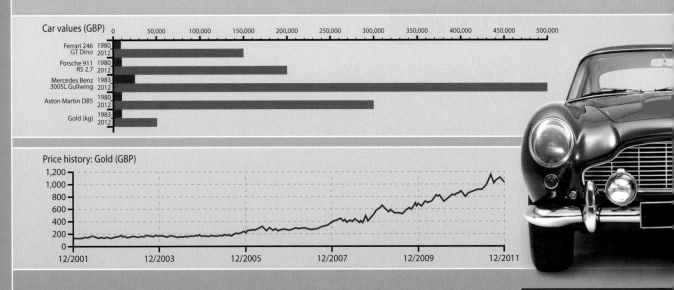

Car values (GBP) — 0, 50,000, 100,000, 150,000, 200,000, 250,000, 300,000, 350,000, 400,000, 450,000, 500,000

- Ferrari 246 GT Dino — 1980, 2012
- Porsche 911 RS 2.7 — 1980, 2012
- Mercedes Benz 300SL Gullwing — 1983, 2012
- Aston Martin DB5 — 1980, 2012
- Gold (kg) — 1983, 2012

Price history: Gold (GBP) — 1,200; 1,000; 800; 600; 400; 200; 0 — 12/2001, 12/2003, 12/2005, 12/2007, 12/2009, 12/2011

5 Answer the questions below using a figure from the article.

1 Approximately how much did gold cost per ounce for the first three years of the decade?
2 What did the price of gold rise to (approximately) in the second half of 2005?
3 At its peak in late 2011, approximately how much did gold cost?
4 How much is an ounce of gold expected to cost in 2020?
5 How much did a Ferrari Dino 246 cost in 1980?
6 What is a Mercedes Benz 300SL worth now?
7 By what percentage has the value of a 1964 Aston Martin DB5 saloon increased?
8 How much did the Aston Martin used in the James Bond films recently sell for?

READING BETWEEN THE LINES

6 Work with a partner. Try to answer the questions below.

1 Why does Warren Buffet dislike gold as an investment?
2 Why are investments in stocks and shares better for society than investing in gold?
3 Why are classic cars a risky investment?

DISCUSSION

7 Work with a partner. Discuss the questions below.

1 Imagine that you and your partner have one million dollars to invest. How would you invest the money?
2 Are there any investments that you definitely would not make? Why would you choose not to invest your money in this way?
3 What investments are popular for people in your country?

READING 2

PREPARING TO READ

1 Work with a partner. Try to answer the questions below.

1 Do you think the standard of living in the USA has increased, decreased or stayed the same since 1950?
2 In what ways do you think the standard of living in the USA has changed? Have these areas got better or worse?
   a the economy   c life expectancy
   b unemployment   d wealth

2 Now read the article below and check your answers.

How times have changed

The American Dream has been described as 'a dream of a land in which life should be better and richer and fuller for everyone'.

This dream became reality for many Americans living in the United States in the 1950s, but are Americans today enjoying the standards of living that their parents and grandparents enjoyed in the post-war years?

After the Second World War, many Americans became richer and their living standards increased as the economy grew. From 1945 to 1973, incomes increased by approximately 3% per year. From the mid-1970s to the mid-1990s, incomes rose very slowly, but then they increased sharply for five years between 1995 and 2000. Overall, incomes have been rising by less and less each year and now the annual increase is almost nothing. However, there is more to living standards than income and spending money.

Job security and unemployment also play a role in the standard of living. Nowadays, factories and offices are closing, which makes jobs less secure. Unemployment, too, is higher than it was in the past. The number of people without a job in the 1950s fell to around 2.5%, but now this figure stands at around 9.5%.

Another measure of the standard of living is the health of the population. Life expectancy is an important measurement of the health in a country. Life expectancy has increased from 68 years in 1950 to 78 today, but the USA is now behind Germany and the United Kingdom (80), France (81) and Japan (82).

One reason for this problem with life expectancy in the United States is obesity, because this has an effect on the general health of the population. In the USA, 35% of adults are obese now, compared with 10% in 1950. This increase is due to the availability and consumption of fast food.

Of course, most Americans own more things than in the post-war years. For example, dishwashers, air conditioning, TVs and phones were only for the richer members of society. Now they can be found in most homes. However, some economists would argue that the standard of living cannot be rising if people are becoming less healthy, or if they cannot afford to retire, or if both parents in a family have to work to pay bills. It seems that although we think we have a better standard of living, this may not be the real picture.

WHILE READING

SKIMMING

UNLOCK
ONLINE

3 Choose the sentence (a–d) that is the best summary of the article.

   a The article discusses the standard of living in the United States compared with other developed countries.

   b The article discusses the factors that should be taken into account when evaluating a country's standard of living.

   c The article discusses the standard of living in the United States now compared with the 1950s.

   d The article discusses how the American Dream became reality for Americans in the post-war years.

Skimming

When we skim a text, we read it quickly to get a general idea of what the text is about, without needing to understand every word.

READING
FOR DETAIL

4 Read the text again and choose the correct statement.

   1 a Incomes rose quickly from 1995 to 2000 but they have been increasing very slowly since then.

     b Incomes rose quickly from 1995 to 2000 but they have been decreasing since then.

   2 a In the 1950s, people felt secure in their jobs because workplaces weren't closing.

     b In the 1950s, people felt secure in their jobs because of the high unemployment rate.

   3 a Life expectancy in the USA is lower than in the United Kingdom, France and Japan but higher than in Germany.

     b Life expectancy in the USA is lower than Germany, the United Kingdom, France and Japan.

   4 a Obesity rates in the USA have risen from 10% to 35% since 1950.

     b Obesity rates in the USA have remained at 35% for over 10 years.

   5 a The standard of living in the USA is better than in the 1950s.

     b The standard of living in the USA is better than in the 1950s in terms of material wealth, but people work hard to achieve it.

READING BETWEEN THE LINES

MAKING
INFERENCES
FROM THE TEXT

5 Work with a partner. Try to answer the questions below.

   1 What factors can improve life expectancy?

   2 What effect does obesity have on life expectancy?

DISCUSSION

6 Work with a partner. Discuss the questions below.

1 How has life in your country changed over the last 60 years?
2 Is the standard of living better or worse now than in the past? Explain your answer.
3 Has your country been affected by an economic crisis? What happened?

⊙ LANGUAGE DEVELOPMENT

ACADEMIC VOCABULARY

1 Use the Glossary on page 197 to find the meanings of the words in the table.

UNL⌀CK ONLINE

noun	adjective
1 economy	economic
2 finance	financial
3 wealth	wealthy
4 poverty	poor
5 manufacturing	manufactured
6 employment	employed
7 profession	professional
8 industry	industrial

2 Complete the sentences (1–8) using either an adjective or a noun from the table in Exercise 1. Each row in the table shows the choices for each sentence.

1 There are major problems with the _____ at the moment.
2 The company is looking to the banks for _____ assistance.
3 Several new internet companies have attracted _____ investors.
4 _____ is still a big problem in parts of the USA.
5 The UK has a smaller _____ sector than Germany.
6 _____ is a big issue for the government because there are not many new jobs.
7 _____ services like legal or financial advice can be expensive.
8 The local area has a long history of heavy _____ with its steel works and chemical plants.

SYNONYMS

3 Match the words (1–6) to their synonyms (a–f).

1 purchase   **a** household
2 income   **b** pay for
3 employee   **c** buyer
4 fund   **d** buy
5 consumer   **e** worker
6 domestic   **f** salary

4 Read the sentences (1–10) below and underline the words from Exercise 3. The first two have been done for you as examples.

1 The money each <u>household</u> owes needs to be reduced.
2 We need to decrease the amount of <u>domestic</u> debt.
3 The state is unable to pay for any further medical facilities.
4 Salaries have not increased for years.
5 The employee bonus scheme means you get more money if you work hard.
6 Buyers should make themselves familiar with their rights when they shop online.
7 The government cannot fund any more new hospitals.
8 There has been no real rise in income lately.
9 Consumers should know their rights when they use online retailers.
10 There are incentives for workers who perform well.

5 Now match the sentences that have the same meaning.

CRITICAL THINKING

At the end of this unit, you will write an explanatory paragraph describing a graph. Look at this unit's Writing task in the box below.

> The graphs show the retail price and annual sales of two different types of television. Describe both graphs and explain the data.

Understanding visual information

Before we can describe a graph or table, we need to make sure we can understand the information.

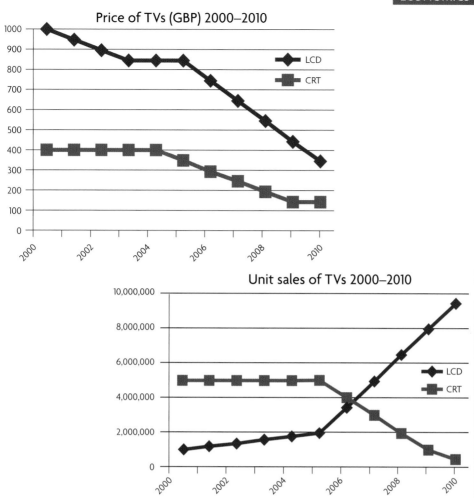

Price of TVs (GBP) 2000–2010

Unit sales of TVs 2000–2010

1 Work with a partner. Look at the graphs above, which show information
   about CRT TVs and LCD TVs, and answer the questions below.

UNDERSTAND

   1 How much did an LCD TV cost:
      a in 2000?   b in 2003?   c in 2005?   d in 2010?
   2 How much did a CRT TV cost:
      a in 2000?   b in 2004?   c in 2009?   d in 2010?
   3 How many LCD TVs were sold:
      a in 2005?   b in 2007?
   4 How many CRT TVs were sold:
      a in 2005?   b in 2007?
   5 In which year were the most LCD TVs sold?
   6 In which year were the fewest CRT TVs sold?

Interpreting visual information

Once we have understood the information, we need to interpret it. This means
identifying relationships between the points on the graph (for example, the
number of sales). In the case of a comparison between two or more sets of
information (in this case, the two different TVs), we also need to identify the
relationships between the sets of data.

2 Work with a partner. Look again at the graph and answer the questions below.

1 Why do you think LCD TVs were so much more expensive than CRT TVs when they were first introduced?

2 Why do you think the prices of both types of TV went down over the period from 2000 to 2010?

3 Which product do you think came on to the market first? Why do you think this?

4 Is there a link between the answers to Questions 5 and 6 in Exercise 1?

5 How many LCD TVs do you think were sold in 2011?

WRITING

GRAMMAR FOR WRITING

UNLOCK ONLINE

1 Match the sentences (1–6) to the graphs (a–f).

1 Sales of TVs rose sharply and then fell dramatically.

2 TV sales decreased slightly and then decreased sharply.

3 The number of TV sales did not change.

4 Television sales increased slightly and then increased sharply.

5 At first, the number of TVs sold did not change but later this figure fluctuated.

6 TV sales fell slightly but did not change after that.

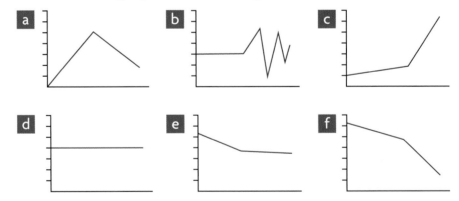

EXPLANATION

Describing graphs - noun phrases and verb phrases

We can describe data with a verb phrase (a verb and an adverb) or a noun phrase (an article, adjective and a noun).

Verb phrase

Sales of TVs **rose sharply** and then **decreased sharply**.

Noun phrase

There was **a sharp rise** in sales of TVs and then **a sharp decrease**.

2 Now write the verb phrases (1–5) as noun phrases. The first one has been done for you as an example.

1 rise sharply   _a sharp rise_
2 fall dramatically   _____
3 decrease slightly   _____
4 increase gradually   _____
5 fluctuate considerably   _____

Prepositions and conjunctions

We use prepositions and conjunctions to add data.

Sales increased sharply **from** 6,000 **to** 7,000 units **between** 2005 **and** 2006.

We use _of_ in a noun phrase to describe the total change.

This was an increase **of** 1,000 units.

3 Complete the sentences below using the words in bold in the examples above.

1 There was a dramatic fall in sales _____ 50 units, _____ 350 _____ 300.
2 Prices rose sharply _____ around 25,000 _____ well over 50,000 – a rise _____ 100%.
3 _____ 2008 _____ 2009, prices decreased slightly _____ £385 _____ £380.
4 Prices fluctuated considerably _____ 2010 _____ 2011.
5 There was a gradual increase in prices _____ £199 _____ £229 in the last six months of the year.

APPROXIMATIONS

4 Which of the words and phrases in the box mean the same? Sort them into three groups.

> almost   nearly   more than   roughly   less than
> over   about   under   approximately   around

5 Match the phrases (1–7) to the figures (a–g).

1 almost a hundred pounds   a £11,156
2 roughly a thousand pounds   b £485,134
3 over ten thousand pounds   c £240,000
4 more than eleven thousand pounds   d £1,014
5 less than a quarter of a million pounds   e £10,237
6 roughly half a million pounds   f £996,001
7 approximately a million pounds   g £99.99

ACADEMIC WRITING SKILLS

WRITING A DESCRIPTION OF A GRAPH

6 Look at the description of a graph below and match the different parts of the paragraph (1–3) to the labels (a–f). Not all the labels are used.

1

> The graph shows the sales figures for two types of mobile phone over an eight-year period.

2

> In year 1, 4,000 units of phone A were sold. Sales of phones increased sharply for the next three years to reach a peak of 20,000, but decreased slightly in year 5. Sales dropped dramatically in years 6 and 7 to 3,000, as a result of the popularity of phone B. In year 8, only 500 units of phone A were sold. Sales of phone B grew more gradually in years 1 and 2 but then in years 3 to 6, there was a dramatic increase in the sales units for the phone as it became well known, until it peaked at 25,000. There was a slight decrease in year 7 but the number of phones sold fell dramatically in year 8 to only 12,000 units.

3

> The graph suggests that sales of phone B will probably drop further in the next year or so.

a Introductory sentence – explains what happened to sales in year one
b Introductory sentence – explains what can be seen on the graph
c Main part of the paragraph – highlights key points
d Main part of the paragraph – explains all the changes
e Concluding sentence – summarizes the changes, predicts what will happen in the future or makes a final comment about the topic of the paragraph
f Concluding sentence – explains the last movements on the graph

WRITING TASK

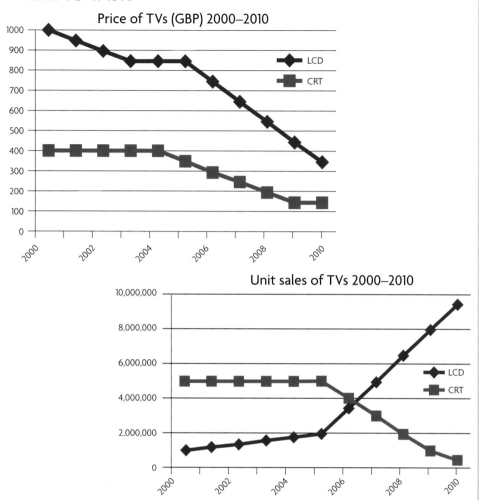

Price of TVs (GBP) 2000–2010

Unit sales of TVs 2000–2010

The graphs show the retail price and annual sales of two different types of television. Describe both graphs and explain the data.

1 Write a description of the two graphs. Write an introductory sentence to say briefly what the graphs show, a main part about the prices and sales, and a concluding sentence summarizing the changes.

WRITE A
FIRST DRAFT

2 Use the task checklist to review your paragraphs for content and structure.

TASK CHECKLIST	✔
Is there an introduction for the graphs?	
Have you described the important information in both graphs and given possible reasons for the changes?	
Have you written a concluding sentence or paragraph?	

3 Make any necessary changes to your paragraphs.

4 Now use the language checklist to edit paragraphs for language errors which are common to B1 learners.

LANGUAGE CHECKLIST	✔
Have you checked the grammar, especially the tenses and prepositions?	
Have you varied your language, using noun phrases, verb phrases and synonyms to describe the topic and the changes?	
Do nouns and verbs agree? Do singular nouns have a singular verb? Do plural nouns have a plural verb?	

5 Make any necessary changes to your paragraphs.

OBJECTIVES REVIEW

6 Check your objectives.

I can ...

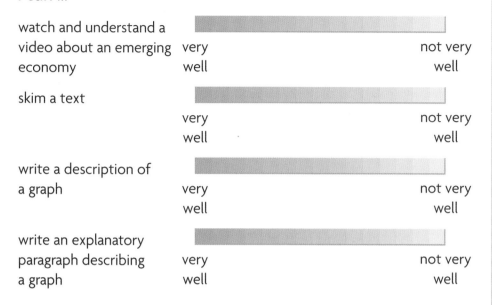

watch and understand a video about an emerging economy	very well	not very well
skim a text	very well	not very well
write a description of a graph	very well	not very well
write an explanatory paragraph describing a graph	very well	not very well

WORDLIST

UNIT VOCABULARY	ACADEMIC VOCABULARY
economic growth (n)	decrease (v)
interest rate (n)	economy (n)
investment (n)	employment (n)
investor (n)	fall (n)
market value (n)	finance (n)
natural resources (n)	increase (v)
precious metal (n)	industry (n)
recession (n)	manufacturing (n)
stocks and shares (n)	poverty (n)
	profession (n)
	rise (v)
	wealth (n)

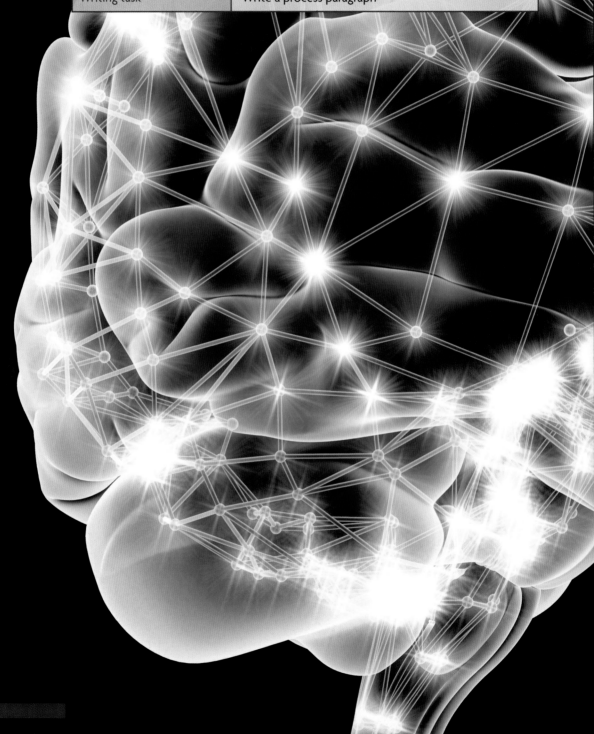

LEARNING OBJECTIVES

Watch and listen	Watch and understand a video about the brain
Reading skills	Preview a text
Academic writing skills	Write a description of a process
Writing task	Write a process paragraph

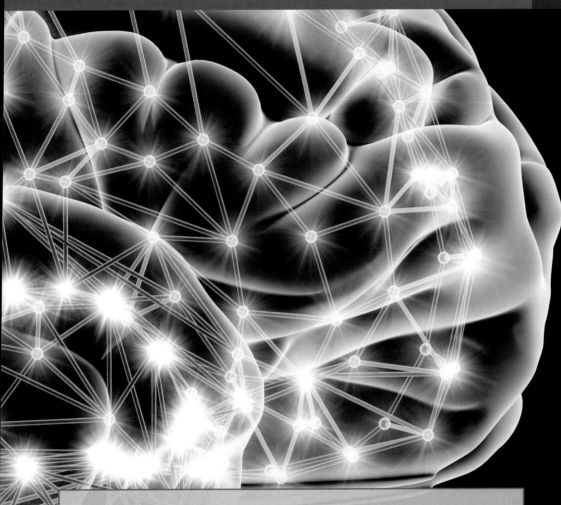

UNLOCK YOUR KNOWLEDGE

How much do you know about the different areas of the brain? Write true (T) or false (F) next to the statements below.

1 The left side of the brain is associated with logic and the right side with creativity. _____

2 The brain uses 20% of the oxygen in the body. _____

3 Only 10% of the brain is used. _____

4 The brain can't feel pain. _____

5 The brain is made up of 90% water. _____

6 Elephants have larger brains than humans. _____

7 Yawning cools down the brain to make it work better. _____

8 The brain stops growing at seven years old. _____

WATCH AND LISTEN

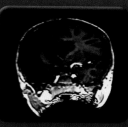

PREPARING TO WATCH

USING YOUR KNOWLEDGE TO PREDICT CONTENT

1 Answer the questions below.

1 What colours are the words below written in?

yellow **blue** **black** **red** orange green **brown**

2 What colours are the words below written in?

red **yellow** **blue** **green** purple **black** orange **white**

3 Which was more difficult to answer – Question 1 or Question 2? Why?

4 What do you think would happen if you lost part of your brain, through an accident or illness?

UNDERSTANDING KEY VOCABULARY

2 Complete the questions below using the words in the box.

> operation   recovery   organ   liquid
> proof   epilepsy   seizures

1 _____ is a condition of the brain which causes a person to become unconscious for short periods or to move in a violent and uncontrolled way.

2 Sudden attacks of uncontrolled movement are called fits or _____ .

3 The brain is surrounded by _____ .

4 _____ of something is a fact that shows something exists or is true.

5 After an _____ , the patient is taken to the _____ room.

6 The brain is an _____ in the body.

WHILE WATCHING

3 ▶ Watch the video and complete the notes using one word for each gap.

- Jody Miller is (1)_____ years old
- has (2)_____ a brain
- after her third birthday (3)_____ took control of her brain
- affected the (4)_____ side of brain
- lost control of the (5)_____ side of body
- seizures might kill Jody: only choice was to (6)_____ out the damaged side
- operation was (7)_____ and careful but a success
- doctors hoped her brain would change and would learn to do (8)_____ for her
- brain changed very (9)_____ and she was able to (10)_____ out of hospital

4 ▶ Watch again. Choose the correct word in the sentences below about the brain.

1 The brain weighs *one and a half kilos / half a kilo* and is the size of a *grapefruit / melon*.
2 The *left / right* side of the brain *controls / operates* the left side of the body.
3 Each half of the brain is split into *three / four* parts, which control thinking, movement and *feeling / feeding*.

5 Work with a partner. Try to answer the questions below.

1 Why is Jody living proof of the amazing power of the brain?
2 How do you think Jody's parents felt before the operation?
3 Why do you think Jody's brain changed so quickly after the operation?
4 Why was it significant that she could walk out of the hospital?

DISCUSSION

6 Work with a partner. Discuss the questions below.

1 What do you think were the risks that Jody's parents had to consider when deciding whether to let their daughter have the operation?
2 How can we look after our brains and exercise them?

PREPARING TO READ

1 Work with a partner. Look at the two sets of photographs in the article, which show two different psychology experiments, and answer the questions.

In the first set of photographs:

1 How many of the people playing with the ball have white T-shirts?

In the second set of photographs:

2 What are the men talking about?
3 Are the men in the first photograph the same as those in the third photograph?
4 Do you think the man giving directions has noticed any change?

Previewing

When we first get a text, it is a good idea to look at the title and any photographs to get an idea of what it is about. This can help us to understand the text, especially if it includes difficult vocabulary or complex ideas.

WHILE READING

2 Read the journal and answer the questions.

1 What did Simons and Chabris want to investigate?

_____

2 What did Simons and Levin want to investigate?

_____

3 What did the results of the experiments show?

_____

Tricks PLAYED BY THE brain

We usually believe what our brain tells us, but there is some amazing evidence which shows that the brain tricks us. As a result, we think we can see something that is not actually there or we ignore things that actually are there.

Psychologists Daniel Simons and Christopher Chabris have researched this phenomenon, which they call 'change blindness'. Their experiments show how we sometimes just do not see what is in front of our eyes because we are concentrating on watching something else.

The 'Invisible Gorilla' experiment is probably their most famous one, and it is described in many psychology textbooks. In this experiment, the participants were shown a video of two groups of people (one group in white T-shirts and one group in black T-shirts) who passed basketballs around in a hallway. Simons and Chabris asked people to count how many times the white team passed the ball. While the two teams were passing their balls around, a person who was dressed up as a gorilla walked through the group and stopped to look at the camera. Simons and Chabris found that approximately half of the research participants did not notice the gorilla.

In another experiment, called the 'Door Study', Simons and Daniel Levin investigated whether people noticed when the person that they were talking to changed! Participants in this study were walking across a university campus when they were stopped by someone they didn't know. The stranger asked for directions and the participant started to give the directions. While the participant was talking to the stranger, two men who were carrying a wooden door walked between the participant and the stranger. At this point, the stranger swapped places with one of the men carrying the door. After that, the participant continued to give the directions and finally, the participant was asked if they had noticed anything change. Once again, about half of those tested did not notice that, when the door was passing by, the stranger had changed places with a man who was taller, thinner and who sounded different. He was also wearing different clothes.

It just goes to show how we can't always trust our own brains. Even though we may think we know what is going on, we can be blind to large changes in our environment.

3 Complete the table using no more than two words for each answer.

experiment	methodology	results
(1)_____	Participants in the experiment watch two teams of people throw a ball around. They have to (2)_____ the number of times the (3)_____ is passed by one of the teams. While this is happening, a (4)_____ walks in front of the camera.	(5)_____ of the participants do not notice the change.
(6)_____	A stranger asks the participant for (7)_____ . While they are talking, two people carrying a (8)_____ walk between them and the (9)_____ changes places with one of the people. The 'new' stranger and the participant then continue talking.	(10)_____ of the participants do not notice that they are talking to someone (11)_____ .

READING BETWEEN THE LINES

4 Try to answer the questions below.

1 What does the writer mean by *participants*?
2 Why do you think people didn't notice that the 'strangers' changed places in the second experiment?

DISCUSSION

5 Work with a partner. Discuss the questions below.

1 Why do you think humans have developed change blindness?
2 Is it important for science lessons in schools to be fun? Why? / Why not?

READING 2

PREPARING TO READ

SCANNING TO PREDICT CONTENT

1 Scan the newspaper article and underline these words each time you find them: *brain*, *technology* and *robotic arm*.

2 Now look at the words you underlined and answer the questions.

   1 Which paragraphs are about the *brain*?

   2 Which paragraphs are about *technology*?

   3 Which paragraphs are about the *robotic arm*?

   4 Which paragraph does not have the word *brain* in it? What is this paragraph about?

MIND CONTROL

A Imagine looking at something and being able to move it just by using your brain! That is exactly what the new technology called BrainGate can do – with the help of a robotic arm, anyway.

B BrainGate is the idea of Professor John Donoghue and his team of researchers at the Brown Institute for Brain Science, in Providence, Rhode Island, USA, who investigate how humans change thoughts in the brain into movements. BrainGate is attached directly to the brain. First of all, gold wires are put into the part of the brain that controls movement. These are then connected to a small computer chip which is just a few millimetres in size. When the person thinks about different movements, this creates electrical signals, which are picked up by the chip. After this, the signals that are created by the brain are sent back to a computer, which changes the signals into movements. Finally, the computer uses the robotic arm to carry out these movements. BrainGate can already be used to write an e-mail, operate the TV remote control or even play computer games, just by brain power.

C The technology is still in the early stages of development but it has already cost millions of dollars to develop and when it is available for use, it will probably cost thousands of dollars per person. There are still many challenges ahead for Donoghue and his team. They are currently planning a mini wireless version of the device, which will allow people to be connected to the computer at all times. Donoghue also dreams of using this technology to help disabled people who can't move their arms and legs. He plans to connect the brain device directly to their own paralysed limbs. This will mean that the person can control their own body again, without relying on a robotic arm. In the near future, he would like to see disabled people feed themselves again and maybe even stand up using BrainGate.

D Clearly, this research could change the lives of disabled people but they are not the only ones who are interested in it. The military think it could be very useful, too. It is easy to understand why scientists might be worried about how thought-controlled machines could be used by the military.

WHILE READING

3 Complete the sentences below about the BrainGate technology. Use no more than three words in each answer.

1 BrainGate was invented by _____ .
2 Metal wires are put into the part of the brain which _____ .
3 When the user thinks of movements, electrical signals are produced and the _____ changes these signals into movements.
4 The movements are carried out by _____ .
5 Donoghue and his team will face a lot of _____ .
6 Governments and the military are also _____ in the technology.

4 Read the article again and write true (T), false (F) or does not say (DNS) next to the statements below.

1 Researchers at the Brown Institute for Brain Science are investigating how movement is controlled by thinking.   _____
2 BrainGate works by reading brain signals and sending the information to a computer chip, which changes the signals into movement.   _____
3 A person with BrainGate can use the robotic arm to make coffee and a sandwich.   _____
4 When the technology is available for use, it is likely to cost around $1,000 per person.   _____
5 There is now also a wireless version of BrainGate.   _____
6 Donoghue says it will be possible to make the perfect soldier using this technology.   _____

READING BETWEEN THE LINES

5 Work with a partner. Try to answer the questions below.

1 How might this technology be used by the military?
2 Why do you think scientists are concerned that the military are interested in this equipment?

DISCUSSION

6 Work with a partner. Discuss the question below.

Do the potential benefits of BrainGate outweigh the risk that people might abuse the technology? Why / Why not?

⊙ LANGUAGE DEVELOPMENT

MEDICAL LANGUAGE

1 Match the nouns (1–10) to their definitions (a–j).

nouns	definitions
1 limb	**a** the treatment of injuries or illness by cutting open the body and repairing it
2 medication	**b** an unwanted effect of a drug that happens in addition to the main effect
3 infectious disease	**c** the movement of an organ from one body to another
4 vaccination	**d** medicine or drugs used to treat an illness
5 surgery	**e** medical care to try to make a patient healthy
6 transplant	**f** something that makes someone with illness healthy again
7 disorder	**g** an injection of a substance that prevents people from getting a disease
8 cure	**h** an illness that is passed from person to person
9 treatment	**i** an arm or leg
10 side-effect	**j** an illness affecting the function of the mind or body

2 Complete the sentences using the nouns in Exercise 1.

1 Stress is a kind of mental _____ .
2 Brain _____ is a very dangerous procedure.
3 Simple things like washing hands can prevent the spread of an
   _____ .
4 Exercise is sometimes seen as a _____ for depression or
   sadness.
5 One _____ of aspirin is stomach bleeding in some
   patients.
6 People who lose a _____ in an accident can be given an
   artificial arm or leg.
7 There is no _____ for some kinds of cancer.
8 Children often receive a _____ against influenza.
9 Most _____ is given in the form of pills or liquids.
10 People who receive a human heart _____ can live for 30
   years after the operation.

3 Work with a partner. Try to answer the questions below.

1 What are the main organs in the human body?
2 How can we control infectious diseases?
3 What is the difference between a treatment and a cure?
4 What are the problems with transplant surgery?

Academic verbs

When we describe a process in academic English, we use a range of
academic verbs.

4 Use the Glossary on page 198 to check the meaning of the verbs in
the box.

recover   carry out   care   complain   advise   confirm   appear

5 Put the sentences in order to describe the treatment of a patient.

a The patient recovers from the operation at home.   _____
b A surgeon arrives to carry out the operation.   _____
c Nurses care for the patient on the recovery ward.   _____
d The patient complains of terrible stomach pain.   _____
e The patient is transferred to a hospital.   _____
f The hospital doctor advises that the patient has their
  appendix removed.   _____
g The hospital doctor confirms that the appendix is diseased. _____
h The family doctor notices the patient appears very ill and
  requires emergency treatment.   _____

CRITICAL THINKING

At the end of this unit, you will write process paragraphs. Look at this unit's Writing task in the box below.

> Write a four-paragraph description of this flow chart, explaining how the body responds to changes in temperature.

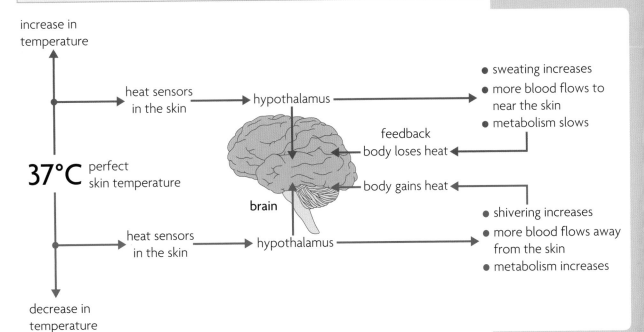

1 Look at the flow chart and match the sentence halves. Use the Wordlist on page 198 to check the meaning of the words.

1 The hypothalamus is an area of the brain which
2 Metabolism means
3 The hypothalamus receives
4 You have less blood near the skin when you are
5 You shiver when your muscles
6 You have more blood near the skin when you are

a chemical reactions in the body that makes fuel from food.
b hot.
c cold.
d signals from heat sensors in the skin.
e contract and relax.
f controls body temperature.

2 Answer the questions about the diagram.

1 Where is the hypothalamus?
2 How does the hypothalamus sense if it is too hot or cold?
3 Why does the hypothalamus need feedback when the body gains or loses heat?
4 What do you think happens if the temperature is too hot or cold for this system to work?

WRITING

GRAMMAR FOR WRITING

EXPLANATION

Passive

We make the passive by moving the topic of the paragraph to the start of the sentence, adding the correct form of be and changing the main verb to the past participle. We add the subject at the end with by or remove it if we don't need it.

The Brown Institute of Brain Science owns BrainGate.
BrainGate is owned by the Brown Institute of Brain Science.

UNLOCK ONLINE

1 Think back to Reading 2. Answer the questions below.

1 Which of the two sentences in the box was used in the article?

> a Scientists attach BrainGate directly to the brain.
> b BrainGate is attached directly to the brain.

2 What is the topic of the entire paragraph, scientists or Braingate?
3 How many of the sentences in the box are in the present tense?

2 Find six more examples of the passive in paragraph B of Reading 2 on page 183.

UNLOCK READING AND WRITING SKILLS 3

3 Change the verbs in the sentences (1–6) into the passive with *be* and the *past participle* to complete the sentences.

1 BrainGate _____ (invent) by Professor John Donoghue.
2 People's brains can _____ (damage) by epilepsy.
3 Language _____ (produce) in two major areas of the brain.
4 The brain can _____ (train) to overcome some hearing loss.
5 Powerful chemicals _____ (release) by the brain when you are stressed.
6 Shivering _____ (increase) in response to a low body temperature.

4 The topic of this unit is the brain. Change the sentences below and use the passive so that the brain is the topic, at the beginning of each sentence.

1 You can fool the brain with simple tricks.

_____

2 People can train the brain to relearn skills after an injury.

_____

3 Forty billion nerve cells make up the brain.

_____

4 Epilepsy interrupts the working of the brain.

_____

5 You can damage your brain in an accident or through disease.

_____

6 Playing music can promote brain development.

_____

ACADEMIC WRITING SKILLS

EXPLANATION

Writing a description of a process

When we describe a process, we need to show the reader the sequence of events in that process. To do this, we use sequencing words and phrases.

to begin with	next
first of all	after that
the first stage/step is	following that
the second stage/step is	finally
then	

1 Read the description of the diagram below and complete it using the words in the box.

> step   shows   However   First   Overall
> After   Next   begin   then   finally

The diagram (1)_____ how the brain controls the amount of water in the body. (2)_____ of all, when the body gets hot, water is lost in sweat. (3)_____ that the hypothalamus in the brain detects that there is not enough water in the blood. (4)_____ the hypothalamus causes the pituitary gland near the brain to release a large amount of a chemical called ADH. The next (5)_____ is when the kidneys remove water from the urine and keep it in the body. (6)_____ , when the body has too much water, the process works the other way. To (7)_____ with, the hypothalamus detects that the blood is too watery, (8)_____ the pituitary gland releases less ADH, and (9)_____ the kidneys lose more water and the water level in the body returns to normal. (10)_____ the diagram shows how complex actions are controlled by the brain, glands and kidneys automatically, without our knowledge.

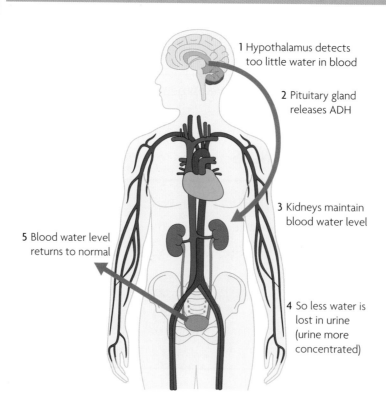

1 Hypothalamus detects too little water in blood

2 Pituitary gland releases ADH

3 Kidneys maintain blood water level

5 Blood water level returns to normal

4 So less water is lost in urine (urine more concentrated)

WRITING TASK

Write a four-paragraph description of this flow chart, explaining how the body responds to changes in temperature.

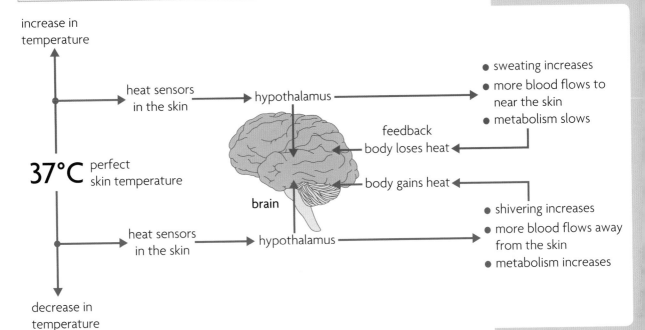

increase in temperature

heat sensors in the skin → hypothalamus
- sweating increases
- more blood flows to near the skin
- metabolism slows

feedback
body loses heat ←

37°C perfect skin temperature

body gains heat ←

brain

heat sensors in the skin → hypothalamus
- shivering increases
- more blood flows away from the skin
- metabolism increases

decrease in temperature

1 Answer the Writing task using information from the Critical thinking section on page 187. Make notes in the space below, then write four paragraphs describing the flow chart.

1 Introduction
2 Say how the body responds to a high temperature.
3 Say how the body responds to a low temperature.
4 Conclusion

WRITE A
FIRST DRAFT

2 Use the task checklist to review your paragraphs for content and structure.

TASK CHECKLIST	✔
Have you introduced the topic by saying what the flow chart shows?	
Have you joined the sentences using sequencing phrases?	
Have you used all the information from the diagram?	

3 Make any necessary changes to your paragraphs.

4 Now use the language checklist to edit your paragraphs for language errors which are common to B1 learners.

LANGUAGE CHECKLIST	✔
Have you used the passive correctly?	
Have you used a range of academic verbs?	
Have you used medical language correctly?	

5 Make any necessary changes to your paragraphs.

OBJECTIVES REVIEW

6 Check your objectives.

I can ...

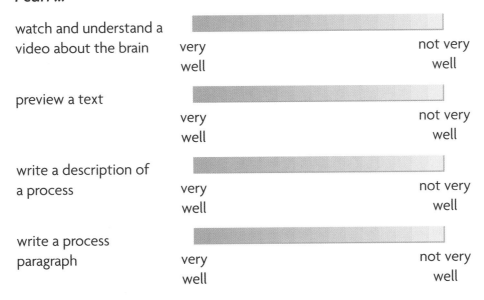

watch and understand a
video about the brain — very well ... not very well

preview a text — very well ... not very well

write a description of
a process — very well ... not very well

write a process
paragraph — very well ... not very well

WORDLIST

UNIT VOCABULARY	ACADEMIC VOCABULARY
cure (n)	advise (v)
disorder (n)	appear (v)
epilepsy (n)	care (n)
liquid (n)	carry out (v)
medication (n)	complain (v)
operation (n)	confirm (v)
proof (n)	recover (v)
recovery (n)	
seizure (n)	
side-effect (n)	
surgery (n)	
treatment (n)	
vaccination (n)	

GLOSSARY

Vocabulary	Pronunciation	Part of speech	Definition
UNIT 1			
aggressive	/əˈgresɪv/	(adj)	behaving in an angry and violent way towards another person
attack	/əˈtæk/	(n)	a violent act intended to hurt or damage someone or something
common	/ˈkɒmən/	(adj)	happening often or existing in large numbers
cruel	/kruəl/	(adj)	extremely unkind and unpleasant and causing pain to people or animals intentionally
endangered	/ɪnˈdeɪndʒəd/	(adj)	animals and plants which may soon disappear from the world because there are very few left alive
extinction	/ɪkˈstɪŋkʃən/	(n)	when a type of animal no longer exists
familiar	/fəˈmɪliə/	(adj)	easy to recognize because of being seen, met, heard, etc. before
fatal	/ˈfeɪtəl/	(adj)	a fatal illness or accident causes death
habitat	/ˈhæbɪtæt/	(n)	the natural environment of an animal or plant
healthy	/ˈhelθi/	(adj)	physically strong and well
hunt	/hʌnt/	(v)	to chase and kill wild animals
hunting	/ˈhʌntɪŋ/	(n)	the sport of chasing and killing animals
overfishing	/ˌəʊvəˈfɪʃɪŋ/	(n)	catching so many fish in a part of the sea that there are not many fish left there
weak	/wik/	(adj)	not physically strong
UNIT 2			
bride	/braɪd/	(n)	a woman who is getting married
brief	/brif/	(adj)	lasting only a short time or using only a few words
certain	/ˈsɜːtən/	(adj)	completely sure of something, or knowing without doubt that something is true
engagement ring	/ɪnˈgeɪdʒmənt rɪŋ/	(n)	a ring usually given by a man to a woman to demonstrate their engagement
fiancé	/fiˈɑ̃nseɪ/	(n)	the man who someone is engaged to be married to
fiancée	/fiˈɑ̃nseɪ/	(n)	the woman who someone is engaged to be married to
groom	/grum/	(n)	a man who is getting married
important	/ɪmˈpɔːtənt/	(adj)	having a lot of power, influence or effect
legal requirement	/ˈligəl rɪˈkwaɪəmənt/	(n)	something you are required to do by law
marriage certificate	/ˈmærɪdʒ səˈtɪfɪkeɪt/	(n)	an official document which records that two people are married
obvious	/ˈɒbviəs/	(adj)	easy to understand or see
punctual	/ˈpʌŋktʃuəl/	(adj)	arriving at the right time and not too late
reception	/rɪˈsepʃən/	(n)	a formal party that is given to celebrate a special event or to welcome someone
registry office	/ˈredʒɪstri ˈɒfɪs/	(n)	in Britain, a place where births, deaths, and marriages are officially recorded and where you can get married
separate	/ˈsepərət/	(adj)	different or new
serious	/ˈsɪəriəs/	(adj)	a serious problem or situation is bad and makes people worry

Vocabulary	Pronunciation	Part of speech	Definition
tend	/tend/	(v)	to look after someone or something
wedding ceremony	/'wedɪŋ 'serɪməni/	(n)	the social event where two people get married
wedding list	/'wedɪŋ 'lɪst/	(n)	a list of presents that a couple who are about to get married have asked to receive

UNIT 3

ancient	/'eɪntʃənt/	(adj)	from a long time ago
archaeologist	/ɑːki'ɒlədʒɪst/	(n)	someone who studies ancient cultures by looking for and examining their buildings, tools, and other objects
archaeology	/ɑːki'ɒlədʒi/	(n)	the study of ancient cultures by looking for and examining their buildings, tools, and other objects
artefact	/'ɑːtɪfækt/	(n)	an object, especially something very old of historical interest
compulsory	/kəm'pʌlsəri/	(adj)	If something is compulsory, you must do it because of a rule or law
display	/dɪ'spleɪ/	(v)	to arrange something somewhere so that people can see it
document	/'dɒkjəment/	(n)	a piece of paper with official information on it
economic	/ikən'ɒmɪk/	(adj)	relating to trade, industry and money
excavation	/ekskə'veɪʃən/	(n)	when earth is removed covering very old objects buried in the ground in order to discover things about the past
exhibit	/ɪg'zɪbɪt/	(n)	an object such as a painting that is shown to the public
exhibition	/eksɪ'bɪʃən/	(n)	when objects such as paintings are shown to the public
field	/'fild/	(n)	an area of study or activity
financial	/faɪ'næntʃəl/	(adj)	relating to money or how money is managed
fossil	/'fɒsəl/	(n)	part of an animal or plant from thousands of years ago, preserved in rock
hieroglyphics	/haɪərəʊ'glɪfɪks/	(n)	a system of writing which uses pictures instead of words, especially used in ancient Egypt
knight	/naɪt/	(n)	a man of high social rank who fought as a soldier on a horse in the past
natural history	/'nætʃərəl 'hɪstəri/	(n)	the study of animals and plants
period	/pɪəriəd/	(n)	a length of time
research	/rɪ'sɜːtʃ/	(v)	to study a subject in detail or to try to find information about a subject
sword	/sɔːd/	(n)	a weapon with a long sharp metal blade and a handle
tuition	/tʃuː'ɪʃən/	(n)	the teaching of one person or of a small group of people

UNIT 4

attempt	/ə'tempt/	(v)	to try to do something, especially something difficult
bus lane	/'bʌs leɪn/	(n)	a special part of the road on which only buses are allowed to travel
carbon-neutral	/kɑːbən njuː'trəl/	(adj)	not producing carbon emissions
congestion charge	/'kəndʒestʃən tʃɑːdʒ/	(n)	the amount of money you have to pay each day to drive into a city centre in order to reduce traffic
consider	/kən'sɪdə/	(v)	to think carefully about something, often before you decide what to do
convince	/kən'vɪnts/	(v)	to persuade someone or make them certain

Vocabulary	Pronunciation	Part of speech	Definition
issue	/ˈɪʃu/	(n)	a subject or problem which people are thinking and talking about
major	/ˈmeɪdʒə/	(adj)	more important, bigger or more serious than others of the same type
outskirts	/ˈaʊtskɜːts/	(n)	the outer area of a city or town
prevent	/prɪˈvent/	(v)	to stop something from happening or someone from doing something
public transport	/pʌblɪk trænt'spɔːt/	(n)	a system of vehicles such as buses and trains which operate at regular times on fixed routes and are used by the public
realize	/ˈrɪəlaɪz/	(v)	to understand a situation
require	/rɪˈkwaɪə/	(v)	to need or demand something
road rage	/ˈrəʊd reɪdʒ/	(n)	anger and violence between drivers
run	/ˈrʌn/	(v)	to organize or control something
rush hour	/ˈrʌʃ aʊə/	(n)	the time when a lot of people are travelling to or from work and so roads and trains are very busy
select	/sɪˈlekt/	(v)	to choose someone or something from a group
traffic congestion	/ˈtræfɪk kəndʒestʃən/	(n)	roads and towns where there is too much traffic and movement is made difficult
vandalism	/ˈvændəlɪzəm/	(n)	the crime of intentionally damaging things in public places
vehicle	/ˈvɪəkəl/	(n)	something such as a car or bus that takes people from one place to another, especially using roads

UNIT 5

annual	/ˈænjuəl/	(adj)	happening once every year, or relating to a period of one year
area	/ˈeəriə/	(n)	a part of a building or piece of land used for a particular purpose
biodiversity	/baɪəʊdaɪˈvɜːsəti/	(n)	the number and types of plants and animals that exist in a particular area
cause	/kɔːz/	(v)	to make something happen, especially something bad
challenge	/ˈtʃælɪndʒ/	(n)	something that is difficult and that tests someone's ability or determination
climate change	/ˈklaɪmət ˈtʃeɪndʒ/	(n)	the way the Earth's weather is changing
consequence	/ˈkɒntsɪkwənts/	(n)	the result of a particular action or situation, especially a bad result
decade	/ˈdekeɪd/	(n)	a period of ten years, especially a period such as 1860 to 1869, or 1990 to 1999
deforestation	/difɒrɪˈsteɪʃən/	(n)	when all the trees in a large area are cut down
drought	/draʊt/	(n)	a long period when there is no rain and people do not have enough water
effect	/ɪˈfekt/	(n)	the result of a particular influence
emission	/iˈmɪʃən/	(n)	when gas, heat, light, etc. is sent out into the air, or an amount of gas, heat, light, etc. that is sent out
erosion	/ɪˈrəʊʒən/	(n)	when soil, stone, etc. is gradually damaged and removed by the sea, rain, or wind
flood	/flʌd/	(n)	a large amount of water covering an area that is usually dry
fossil fuel	/ˈfɒsəl fjuəl/	(n)	fuels such as gas, coal and oil that were formed underground from plant and animal remains millions of years ago
glacier	/ˈglæsiə/	(n)	a large mass of ice that moves very slowly, usually down a slope or valley

Vocabulary	Pronunciation	Part of speech	Definition
global warming	/ˈgləʊbəl ˈwɔːmɪŋ/	(n)	a gradual increase in world temperatures caused by polluting gases
graze	/greɪz/	(v)	when cows or other animals graze, they eat grass
greenhouse gas	/ˈgriːnhaʊs ˈgæs/	(n)	a gas that causes the greenhouse effect, especially carbon dioxide
issue	/ˈɪʃu/	(n)	a subject or problem which people are thinking and talking about
predict	/prɪˈdɪkt/	(v)	to say that an event or action will happen in the future, especially as a result of knowledge or experience
submerge	/səbˈmɜːdʒ/	(v)	to cause something to be under the surface of water, or to move below the surface of water
subsistence farming	/səbˈsɪstəns fɑːmɪŋ/	(n)	farming that provides enough food for the farmer and their family to live on but not enough for them to sell
environment	/ɪnvˈaɪərənmənt/	(n)	the air, land and water where people, animals and plants live
trend	/ˈtrend/	(n)	a general development or change in a situation or in the way that people are behaving

UNIT 6

Vocabulary	Pronunciation	Part of speech	Definition
balanced diet	/ˈbæləntst daɪət/	(n)	a combination of the correct types and amounts of food
calorie	/ˈkæləri/	(n)	a unit for measuring the amount of energy food provides
education	/edʒʊˈkeɪʃən/	(n)	the process of teaching or learning in a school or college, or the knowledge that you get from this
encourage	/ɪnˈkʌrɪdʒ/	(v)	to make someone more likely to do something, or to make something more likely to happen
evidence	/ˈevɪdənts/	(n)	something that makes you believe that something is true or exists
exercise	/ˈeksəsaɪz/	(n)	physical activity that you do to make your body strong and healthy
government	/ˈgʌvənmənt/	(n)	the group of people who officially control a country
heart disease	/ˈhɑːt dɪˈziz/	(n)	a medical condition affecting the heart
individual	/ɪndɪˈvɪdʒuəl/	(n)	a person, especially when considered separately and not as part of a group
injure	/ˈɪndʒə/	(v)	to hurt a person, animal or part of your body
involve	/ɪnˈvɒlv/	(v)	if a situation or activity involves something, that thing is a necessary part of it
junk food	/ˈdʒʌŋk fud/	(n)	food which is unhealthy but which is quick and easy to eat
life expectancy	/ˈlaɪf ɪkspˈektəntsi/	(n)	the number of years that someone is likely to live
obesity	/əʊˈbisəti/	(n)	the state of being extremely fat
provide	/prəʊˈvaɪd/	(v)	to give someone something that they need
realize	/ˈrɪəlaɪz/	(v)	to notice or understand something that you did not notice or understand before
reduce	/rɪˈdʒus/	(v)	to make something less
self-esteem	/self ɪˈstim/	(n)	confidence in yourself and a belief in your qualities and abilities
solve	/ˈsɒlv/	(v)	to find the answer to something
suffer	/ˈsʌfə/	(v)	to experience something bad

UNIT 7

Vocabulary	Pronunciation	Part of speech	Definition
advantage	/ədˈvɑːntɪdʒ/	(n)	something good about a situation that helps you
benefit	/ˈbenɪfɪt/	(n)	something that helps you or gives you an advantage
biofuel	/ˈbaɪəʊ fjuəl/	(n)	fuel produced from plant material

Vocabulary	Pronunciation	Part of speech	Definition
centre of gravity	/ˈsentə ɒv ɡrævəti/	(n)	the point in an object where its weight is balanced
concern	/kənˈsɜːn/	(n)	when you feel worried or nervous about something, or something that makes you feel worried
definitely	/ˈdefɪnətli/	(adv)	without any doubt
disability	/dɪsəˈbɪləti/	(n)	an illness, injury or condition that makes it difficult for someone to do the things that other people do
disadvantage	/dɪsədˈvɑːntɪdʒɪz/	(n)	something which makes a situation more difficult, or makes you less likely to succeed
discovery	/dɪˈskʌvəri/	(n)	when someone discovers something
genetic modification	/ˈdʒɜːnetɪk mɒdɪfɪˈkeɪʃən/	(n)	when biological cells are changed in order to make an animal or plant healthier or more useful to humans
gesture	/ˈdʒestʃə/	(n)	a movement you make with your hand, arm, or head to express what you are thinking or feeling
innovation	/ɪnəʊˈveɪʃən/	(n)	a new idea or method that is being tried for the first time, or the use of such ideas or methods
possibly	/ˈpɒsəbli/	(adv)	something is not certain
probably	/ˈprɒbəbli/	(adv)	mean that something is very likely
scientific	/saɪəntˈɪfɪk/	(adj)	relating to science, or using the organized methods of science
UNIT 8			
accommodate	/əˈkɒmədeɪt/	(v)	to do what someone needs, often by providing them with something
approach	/əˈprəʊtʃ/	(n)	a way of doing something
area	/ˈeəriə/	(n)	a part of a building or piece of land used for a particular purpose
artificial fibres	/ɑːtɪˈfɪʃəl faɪbəz/	(n)	man-made thread-like materials from plants which can be made into cloth
beauty products	/ˈbjuti prɒdʌkts/	(n)	soap, make-up and creams used to make people more beautiful
brief	/ˈbrif/	(adj)	lasting only a short time or using only a few words
casual clothes	/ˈkæʒjuəl kləʊðz/	(n)	ordinary clothes worn when not working
consumption	/kənˈsʌmpʃən/	(n)	the amount of something that someone uses, eats, or drinks
drama	/ˈdrɑːmə/	(n)	an event or situation, especially an unexpected one, in which there is worry or excitement and usually a lot of action
employee	/ɪmˈplɔɪi/	(n)	someone who is paid to work for someone else
goal	/ɡəʊl/	(n)	an aim or purpose
manufacturing plant	/ˈmænjəfæktʃərɪŋ plɑːnt/	(n)	a factory or a building where goods are produced in large numbers
multinational company	/mʌltiˈnæʃənəl kʌmpəni/	(n)	a business that operates in, produces goods in, or sells its products in several different countries
natural fibres	/ˈnætʃərəl faɪbəz/	(n)	thread-like materials from plants which can be made into cloth
relax	/rɪˈlæks/	(v)	to become happy and comfortable because nothing is worrying you, or to make someone do this
textile	/ˈtekstaɪl/	(n)	a cloth made by hand or machine
volume	/ˈvɒljum/	(n)	the number or amount of something, especially when it is large

Vocabulary	Pronunciation	Part of speech	Definition
UNIT 9			
decrease	/dɪˈkriːs/	(v)	to become less, or to make something become less
economic growth	/ikənˈɒmɪk grəʊθ/	(n)	an increase in the economy of a country or an area
economy	/ikˈɒnəmi/	(n)	the system by which a country produces and uses goods and money
employment	/ɪmˈplɔɪmənt/	(n)	when someone is paid to work for a company or organization
fall	/fɔːl/	(n)	when the size, amount or strength of something gets lower
finance	/ˈfaɪnænts/	(n)	the control of how large amounts of money should be spent
increase	/ɪnˈkriːs/	(v)	to get bigger or to make something bigger in amount or size
industry	/ˈɪndəstri/	(n)	the people and activities involved in one type of business
interest rate	/ˈɪntrəst reɪts/	(n)	the interest percent that a bank charges you when you borrow money, or the interest it pays you when you keep money in an account
investment	/ɪnˈvestmənt/	(n)	the money that you put in a bank, business, etc. in order to make a profit, or the act of doing this
investor	/ɪnˈvestə/	(n)	a person who puts money into a bank, business, etc. in order to make a profit
manufacturing	/mænjəfˈæktʃərɪŋ/	(n)	the business of producing goods in large numbers
market value	/ˈmɑːkɪt vælju/	(n)	the price that something could be sold for at a particular time
natural resources	/nætʃərəl rɪˈzɔːsɪz/	(n)	things such as minerals, forests, coal, etc. which exist in a place and can be used by people
poverty	/ˈpɒvəti/	(n)	the condition of being extremely poor
precious metal	/preʃəs meˈtəl/	(n)	a metal like gold or silver that is valuable and usually rare
profession	/prəfˈeʃən/	(n)	a type of work that needs special training or education
recession	/rɪˈseʃən/	(n)	a period when the economy of a country is not successful and conditions for business are bad
rise	/raɪz/	(v)	to increase in level
stocks and shares	/ˈstɒks ænd ˈʃeəz/	(n)	financial investments in a company or a supply of goods
wealth	/ˈwelθ/	(n)	a large amount of money or valuable possessions that someone has
UNIT 10			
advise	/ədˈvaɪz/	(v)	to make a suggestion about what you think someone should do or how they should do something
appear	/əˈpɪə/	(v)	to seem
care	/keə/	(n)	the process of protecting and looking after someone or something
carry out	/kæri ˈaʊt/	(v)	to do or complete something
complain	/kəmˈpleɪn/	(v)	to say that something is wrong or that you are annoyed about something
confirm	/kənˈfɜːm/	(v)	to say or show that something is true
cure	/kjʊə/	(n)	something that makes someone with an illness healthy again
disorder	/dɪˈsɔːdə/	(n)	an illness or medical condition
epilepsy	/ˈepɪlepsi/	(n)	a brain disease which can make someone become unconscious and have fits

Vocabulary	Pronunciation	Part of speech	Definition
liquid	/ˈlɪkwɪd/	(n)	a substance, such as water, that is not solid or a gas and that can be poured easily
medication	/medɪˈkeɪʃən/	(n)	medicine that is used to treat an illness
operation	/ɒpərˈeɪʃən/	(n)	when a doctor cuts someone's body to remove or repair part of it
proof	/pruf/	(n)	a fact or a piece of information that shows something exists or is true
recover	/rɪˈkʌvə/	(v)	to become healthy or happy again after an illness, injury, or period of sadness
recovery	/rɪˈkʌvəri/	(n)	when you feel better or happier again after an illness, injury, or period of sadness
seizure	/ˈsiʒə/	(n)	a sudden attack of an illness
side-effect	/ˈsaɪd ɪˈfekt/	(n)	another effect that a drug has on your body in addition to the main effect for which the doctor has given you the drug
surgery	/ˈsɜːdʒəri/	(n)	when a doctor cuts your body open and repairs or removes something
treatment	/ˈtritmənt/	(n)	the use of drugs, exercises, etc. to cure a person of an illness or injury
vaccination	/væksɪˈneɪʃən/	(n)	an injection that protects you against a disease

VIDEO SCRIPT

UNIT 1 SHARKS

Narrator: The great white shark is known for its size. The largest sharks can grow to six metres in length and over 2,000 kilograms in weight. Great white sharks are meat-eaters and prey on large sea creatures like tuna, seals and even whales. Great whites have also been known to attack boats. This researcher is lucky to escape with his life when a shark bites into his boat. Three people are killed on average each year by great white sharks.

This is False Bay, South Africa, one of the best places in the world to see a great white. The sharks come to hunt the 60,000 seals that live here. In order to find fish, the seals have to cross the deep water of the bay – this is where the sharks wait. Great whites are expert hunters and take prey by surprise from below. They wait underneath the seals and then swim up and crash into them at 40 kilometres per hour, killing them with one bite.

These scientists are trying to find out how sharks choose what to attack. Will a shark attack something that looks like food? See how the sharks react when researchers put carpet in the shape of a seal in the water. At high speeds the shark can't tell the difference.

Can a shark choose between a plant and a fish? When scientists put tuna and seaweed in the water, the shark bites into both. Even though sharks eat meat, if a plant looks like an animal, the shark attacks.

Will a shark prefer to eat a human or a fish? When the shark has a choice between humans and tuna, it is the fish that attracts the shark's attention. Great white sharks clearly prefer fish to humans.

The research these scientists are doing shows that great white sharks are dangerous hunters which will attack anything that looks and acts like a fish. Unfortunately, that means humans can also get bitten by mistake.

UNIT 2 CUSTOMS

Narrator: Dagestan is a land of towering mountains, rushing rivers and ancient stone villages. Dagestan is an amazing mix of ethnic and cultural diversity. About thirty-five separate groups live side by side in this republic, which is the size of Scotland or the UAE.

Dagestan is the southernmost region of the Russian Federation, where the people speak an amazing 12 languages. Traditions are respected all over Dagestan and particularly in the rural areas, where little has changed for generations.

These women are making traditional Dagestani carpets. Everything is done by hand, with designs that are hundreds of years old. All the materials are local, from the wool used to make thread, to the dyes made from local roots and vegetables. The carpets are sold around the world and can be seen in many major museums.

Respecting the elderly members of the community is very important in Dagestani culture. Older people are local leaders in the special system of family networks in Dagestan.

The population is growing fast in Dagestan. People have large families. Even though many Dagestanis now live outside the country, it is common for people to return to their family home when they get older. Most Dagestanis say they would like to be buried in their home village in the mountains, as their families have done for hundreds of years.

UNIT 3 ARCHAEOLOGY

Narrator: Wonderful artwork, ancient writing, and huge stone monuments. These are the remains of ancient Egyptian civilization which have amazed the world for centuries.

Egyptology was born in 1799, when the ancient Egyptian writing system – hieroglyphics – was first translated. Today, the archaeological season in Egypt starts in October, when a small number of archaeologists are allowed to start excavations. It is illegal to excavate or remove artefacts without permission, and security is tight.

These are the tombs of the ancient kings of Egypt. Down the dark passages, there are many clues about ancient Egyptian society. Complicated rituals surrounded death, and fantastic treasure was buried for use in the afterlife. Hidden underground, these painted tombs and fragile artefacts have been preserved by the dry air of the desert.

Before any discoveries can be made, there is always a large amount of earth and sand to move first. In the ancient city of Thebes, a team of archaeologists work to remove the sand that has hidden a tomb for two and a half thousand years. It is a time-consuming task but the site is so delicate, heavy machinery is not allowed and the earth must be moved by hand.

On the other side of the river Nile, in the Valley of the Kings, another team of archaeologists use the latest X-ray equipment to examine a mummy. The equipment can show the age, gender and cause of death of the mummy without damaging the fragile remains. The excavation is examined very closely. Every new artefact must be carefully recorded and nothing can be moved until it is photographed and preserved by experts. Every year, archaeologists continue to look for more evidence of this advanced culture under the hot Egyptian sun.

UNIT 4 INDIAN TRANSPORT

Narrator: For a country with a population of 1.2 billion, there are only 13 million cars in India. Some traditional forms of transport have been in use in India for centuries. Water taxis take thousands of passengers along the river Ganges every day. The wooden boats they use are handed from father to son, and the boat men repair them themselves.

Ox carts have been traditionally used for transport, especially in rural India. In recent years, some cities have banned the movement of ox carts and other slow-moving vehicles on the main roads because of traffic problems.

Bicycles are a common mode of travel in much of India. More people can now afford to own a bicycle than ever before. In 2005, more than 40% of Indian households owned a bicycle. But for long journeys, public transport is essential and India's public transport systems are among the most heavily used in the world.

Railways were first introduced to India in 1853. By 1947, there were 42 rail systems. In 1951, the systems were nationalized as one unit, becoming one of the largest networks in the world. With 65,000 kilometres of rail routes and 7,500 stations, the railway network in India is the fourth biggest in the world after Russia, China and the USA. Indian trains carry over 30 million passengers and 2.8 million tonnes of freight daily.

Indian Railways are the world's biggest employer, with over 1.4 million staff. Generally, Indian Railways are very efficient, but trains do run late, and sometimes it is hours rather than minutes. However, at the moment, they are a much better option than a traffic jam.

UNIT 5 GLOBAL WARMING

Narrator: The frozen glaciers of Alaska have remained unchanged for millions of years. But now the ice is melting and the impact on our environment will be huge. These ice sheets start life as snow, turn to glaciers, and eventually crash into the sea. A single glacier can move up to a metre every hour.

An astonishing 20,000 trillion tonnes of ice move across Alaska every day. Alaska's 100,000 glaciers are under threat of disappearing because they are very sensitive to the effects of global warming. To understand why, adventurer Will Gadd is going where few have gone before: to follow one of the melt streams running through the glacier.

These fast rivers of freezing water are formed as glaciers melt, and they are an important measure of its health. Every glacier is in balance. The amount of snow falling in winter must equal the amount that melts in the summer. If that balance changes, the glacier will disappear. Right now, that's what's happening. These glaciers are melting faster than they are growing.

Alaskan glaciers have been here for over three million years. They are currently losing ice at the rate of 80 billion tonnes a year. It's the end of the road for this glacier as it tumbles off the mountains and into the sea.

Alaska's glaciers are retreating at an increasing rate. Every year, 19 trillion tonnes of melt water are pouring away and not being replenished. As the glaciers melt away, it's the rest of the world that's affected. Alaskan glaciers are melting so fast, they are accounting for ten percent of the world's rising sea levels. It's the most dramatic transformation this area has undergone since the ice age and shows how global warming is changing our environment. It's hard to believe all this could soon be gone.

UNIT 6 CYCLING

Narrator: The world's top road cyclists manage to ride for over three and a half thousand kilometres, at an average speed of 40 kilometres per hour, in each race. How do they manage this amazing physical achievement?

Teams who compete at the highest level in the Tour de France put their success down to training. The riders in the team treat their training for any sport as if it is a job. For example, they set goals for each day's training and, like a regular job, they stop when they reach these goals. This means even though they might cycle 700 kilometres a week, they don't train too hard and get injured before their race.

The way they train means that they are much fitter than a normal person. The best riders extract twice as much oxygen from each breath as an average healthy person, so they are able to generate twice as much energy. Riders like this train their hearts to pump nine gallons of blood to their muscles per minute, whereas you or I could only manage five.

The team of riders is built entirely around helping the team leader win the race. The team work together to make sure that the leader is fresh to cycle fastest at the end of the race.

The team's job is to block the wind that he rides into. They ride in a V-shape, so that the leader can save a quarter of the energy he would normally spend riding into the wind. In a side wind, the team ride in a wing shape to protect him.

The team also make sure that their equipment and food is the most advanced. Modern bicycles use space technology and weigh 1.3 kilograms. A wind tunnel is used to analyze a rider's position on the bike and reduce drag. To get the most energy for the race, cyclists train their body to burn fat by not eating too many carbohydrates, but as they start to race, they eat a lot more. During a race, a cyclist can consume up to 4,000 calories per day in carbohydrates alone.

This kind of preparation is the key to winning a race that can last up to three weeks. Even the smallest aspect of a rider's performance could be the difference between winning and losing.

UNIT 7 ROBOTS

Narrator: Robots are very different from the Hollywood version. They are widely used today in factories, in space, and deep under water for jobs which are too dirty, boring or dangerous for humans to do.

Meet ASIMO. In 1986, the Honda automotive company wanted to see if it could make a humanoid robot that could act like we do, to help in the home, play football, balance on one foot, and even dance. Over the years there were some problems but soon the researchers managed to get a robot that could walk on uneven surfaces, and shift its centre of gravity like we do to climb stairs. More recently, ASIMO was improved so it could turn round and run at six kilometres per hour, using its upper body to control movement.

ASIMO is designed to be people-friendly. It is hoped that robots like this could be used to help elderly people in their home. Honda are also using this technology to create mobility aids for people with disabilities. It can also push a cart and open and close doors.

ASIMO can even shake hands and recognize gestures. It stands 120 centimetres tall, so that it can look into adult faces when they are sitting down. It can hold two kilograms in its hands and carry a tray without dropping the contents.

So, where next for this kind of robot? Well, while ASIMO is physically impressive, it is still controlled by a human. Researchers in the USA are working on robots that can learn about the world around them, and respond to human touch and voice. The robots are even learning to recognize objects, people and vocabulary.

Soon the descendents of these robots may be serving you drinks or helping with jobs at home and at work.

UNIT 8 MISSONI FASHION

Narrator: Milan is in the Lombardy region in the north of Italy. It is Italy's second biggest city and one of the great fashion capitals of the world. Like London, Paris and New York, twice a year Milan has Fashion Week.

The fashion industry is worth six billion dollars a year. Angela Missoni is a fashion designer. Her label, Missoni, is one of the most famous, but it has not been easy to be a successful fashion label. The Missoni label was started in 1953 in a one-bedroom flat by Angela's parents, Ottavio and Rosita.

Angela runs the business with her brothers, Vittorio and Luca.

Eight hundred people work in Missoni's factories, helping to produce the label's popular collections. Their company now makes more than 250 million dollars a year.

Angela is busy preparing for Milan Fashion Week. Milan Fashion Week has started. Critics, journalists and buyers come to the city from around the world.

Angela is making last-minute preparations. She has to choose which dresses to include in the show. Finally, the show starts. Fashion Week is a great success.

UNIT 9 RUSSIA'S ECONOMIC SUCCESS

Narrator: When the Soviet Union fell in 1991, Russia's economy suffered major difficulties. For the next decade, the country went from financial crisis to financial crisis. Foreign investors stayed away, and there was a rapid decline in the value of the Russian currency, the rouble.

Since then, the Russian economy has grown at an average of seven percent a year, and the country has one of the strongest stock markets in the world. Global investment banks describe Russia's economic performance as 'remarkable'.

So how did Russia turn a failing economy into a financial powerhouse? The oil wealth created a lot of very rich people. These people invested in industries after the fall of the Soviet Union, and now Russia has over one hundred billionaires and Moscow has more than any other city in the world. But it's not only the rich in Russia who are benefitting from the oil. Retail sales are growing, and multinational companies are now competing to invest in Russia.

New shopping malls are now spreading beyond Moscow to the rest of Russia. However, there is a problem with relying on natural resources for economic growth. The oil is running out fast. It is predicted that the oil will only last for another 30 to 40 years. However, Russian oil has restarted an economy which was in crisis and brought wealth and economic stability to the country.

UNIT 10 THE BRAIN

Narrator: This organ – one and a half kilograms of fat, the size of a grapefruit – holds all the secrets of what makes us human. It is the most complicated object in the known universe.

Young Jody Miller is living proof of the brain's amazing abilities. She has a normal life as a nine-year-old school girl. You would never guess that she only has half a brain.

Jody's first three years were normal but a few weeks after her third birthday, something started to go wrong. Epilepsy took control of her brain.

They found that she was suffering from storms of electricity in her right brain. Seizures happened all the time, and she lost control of the left side of her body. Doctors became worried that the epileptic seizures might kill Jody. The doctors and Jody's parents were left with one choice: to take out the damaged side of her brain.

Our brains are made of two different sides, each split into four parts. Parts on both sides control thinking, movement and feeling. The right side controls the left side of the body, and the left side controls the right. Jody would lose all of the right side of her brain. The space would then fill up with liquid.

The operation was slow and careful but it was a success. Doctors hoped that Jody's brain would change shape, and the left side of the brain would learn to do everything for Jody. Her brain started to change very quickly and she was able to walk out of the hospital. Jody's recovery is proof of the amazing power of the brain.

ACKNOWLEDGEMENTS

Author acknowledgements

I would like to thank the publishing team at Cambridge University Press, especially my editor, Barry Tadman for his unending patience and advice throughout the writing process. Thanks are also due to Lyn Strutt for editing the proofs. I would also like to thank all my friends and family for their support, in particular, my husband, Kevin, who supports me in everything I do and my lovely sons, Kai and Christian, for being so understanding when work had to take precedence over play. I would also like to thank my mother, Vera, and my mother-in-law, Kath, for always being there to help and support me in everything I do.
Carolyn Westbrook

Publisher's acknowledgements

The publishers are extremely grateful to the following people and their students for reviewing and trialling this course during its development. The course has benefited hugely from your insightful comments, advice and feedback.

Mr M.K. Adjibade, King Saud University, Saudi Arabia; Canan Aktug, Bursa Technical University, Turkey; Olwyn Alexander, Heriot Watt University, UK; Valerie Anisy, Damman University, Saudi Arabia; Anwar Al-Fetlawi, University of Sharjah, UAE; Laila Al-Qadhi, Kuwait University, Kuwait; Tahani Al-Taha, University of Dubai, UAE; Ozlem Atalay, Middle East Technical University, Turkey; Seda Merter Ataygul, Bursa Technical University Turkey; Harika Altug, Bogazici University, Turkey; Kwab Asare, University of Westminster, UK; Erdogan Bada, Cukurova University, Turkey; Cem Balcikanli, Gazi University, Turkey; Gaye Bayri, Anadolu University, Turkey; Meher Ben Lakhdar, Sohar University, Oman; Emma Biss, Girne American University, UK; Dogan Bulut, Meliksah University, Turkey; Sinem Bur, TED University, Turkey; Alison Chisholm, University of Sussex, UK; Dr. Panidnad Chulerk , Rangsit University, Thailand; Sedat Cilingir, Bilgi University, Istanbul, Turkey; Sarah Clark, Nottingham Trent International College, UK; Elaine Cockerham, Higher College of Technology, Muscat, Oman; Asli Derin, Bilgi University, Turkey; Steven Douglass, University of Sunderland, UK; Jacqueline Einer, Sabanci University, Turkey; Basak Erel, Anadolu University, Turkey; Hande Lena Erol, Piri Reis Maritime University, Turkey; Gulseren Eyuboglu, Ozyegin University, Turkey; Muge Gencer, Kemerburgaz University, Turkey; Jeff Gibbons, King Fahed University of Petroleum and Minerals, Saudi Arabia; Maxine Gilway, Bristol University, UK; Dr Christina Gitsaki, HCT, Dubai Men's College, UAE; Sam Fenwick, Sohar University, Oman; Peter Frey, International House, Doha, Qatar; Neil Harris, Swansea University, UK; Vicki Hayden, College of the North Atlantic, Qatar; Joud Jabri-Pickett, United Arab Emirates University, Al Ain, UAE; Aysel Kilic, Anadolu University, Turkey; Ali Kimav, Anadolu University, Turkey; Bahar Kiziltunali, Izmir University of Economics, Turkey; Kamil Koc, Ozel Kasimoglu Coskun Lisesi, Turkey; Ipek Korman-Tezcan, Yeditepe University, Turkey; Philip Lodge, Dubai Men's College, UAE; Iain Mackie, Al Rowdah University, Abu Dhabi, UAE; Katherine Mansfield, University of Westminster, UK; Kassim Mastan, King Saud University, Saudi Arabia; Elspeth McConnell, Newham College, UK; Lauriel Mehdi, American University of Sharjah, UAE; Dorando Mirkin-Dick, Bell International Institute, UK; Dr Sita Musigrungsi, Prince of Songkla University, Hatyai, Thailand; Mark Neville, Al Hosn University, Abu Dhabi, UAE; Shirley Norton, London School of English, UK; James Openshaw, British Study Centres, UK; Hale Ottolini, Mugla Sitki Kocman University, Turkey; David Palmer, University of Dubai, UAE; Michael Pazinas, United Arab Emirates University, UAE; Troy Priest, Zayed University, UAE; Alison Ramage Patterson, Jeddah, Saudi Arabia; Paul Rogers, Qatar Skills Academy, Qatar; Josh Round, Saint George International, UK; Harika Saglicak, Bogazici University, Turkey; Asli Saracoglu, Isik University, Turkey; Neil Sarkar, Ealing, Hammersmith and West London College, UK; Nancy Shepherd, Bahrain University, Bahrain; Jonathan Smith, Sabanci University, Turkey; Peter Smith, United Arab Emirates University, UAE; Adem Soruc, Fatih University Istanbul, Turkey; Dr Peter Stanfield, HCT, Madinat Zayed & Ruwais Colleges, UAE; Maria Agata Szczerbik, United Arab Emirates University, Al Ain, UAE; Burcu Tezcan-Unal, Bilgi University, Turkey; Dr Nakonthep Tipayasuparat, Rangsit University, Thailand; Scott Thornbury, The New School, New York, USA; Susan Toth, HCT, Dubai Men's Campus, Dubai, UAE; Melin Unal, Ege University, Izmir, Turkey; Aylin Unaldi, Bogaziçi University, Turkey; Colleen Wackrow, Princess Nourah bint Abdulrahman University, Riyadh, Saudi Arabia; Gordon Watts, Study Group, Brighton UK; Po Leng Wendelkin, INTO at University of East Anglia, UK; Halime Yildiz, Bilkent University, Ankara, Turkey; Ferhat Yilmaz, Kahramanmaras Sutcu Imam University, Turkey.

Special thanks to Peter Lucantoni for sharing his expertise, both pedagogical and cultural.

Photo acknowledgements

The authors and publishers acknowledge the following sources of copyright material and are grateful for the permissions granted. While every effort has been made, it has not always been possible to identify the sources of all the material used, or to trace all copyright holders. If any omissions are brought to our notice, we will be happy to include the appropriate acknowledgements on reprinting.

p.12: (1) © Eric Limon/Shutterstock; p.12: (2) © szefai/Shutterstock; p.12: (3) © Steven Vidler/Eurasia Press/Corbis; pp.14/15: © Nir Elia/Reuters/Corbis; p.20(L&R): Shutterstock; p.32/33: © Joes Fuste Raga/Corbis; p.36(B): Tokyo Spakce Club/Corbis; p.36(C): © Kim Steele/Blend Images/Corbis; p.36(T): Getty Images; p.50/51: Design Pics/Corbis; p.55(TL): Marques/Shutterstock; p.55(R): © Andrew Fox/Corbis; p.55(CL): © Iain Masterton/Alamy; p.55(BR): Jian Xintong Xinhau Pictures/Corbis; p.68/69: © Keren Su/China epa; p.72(TL): Getty Images; p.72(TR): Kevpix/Alamy; p.73(BR): Getty Images; p.75(TL): © Peet Simard/Corbis; p.75(TC): © Pawel Libera/Corbis; p.75(R): © Aaron Yeoman/Getty Images; p.86/87: © Paul Souders/Corbis; p.91: © Daniel Beltra/Archivo Museo Salesiano/Greenpeace; p.94: © Cyril Rueso/J H Editorial/Minden Pictures/Corbis; p.104/105: © Raphael Christinat/Shutterstock; p.108 (1): Images Source/Corbis; p.108(5): Fancy/Corbis; p.108(3): © John Lund/Marc Romanelli/Blend Images/Corbis; p.108(2): Images Source/Corbis; p.108(6): Lightpoet/Shutterstock; p.108(7): © Tom Wang/Alamy; p.108(4):© Eric Ardas/Corbis; p.108(8): © Khalid Eifiqui/epa/Corbis; p.122/123: Honda UK; p.127(BR): Cloud Hill Images Ltd/Science Photo Library: p.127(R): Eye of Science/Science Photo Library; p.127(BL): © James Davies; p.129(L): © Kimmasa Mauama/Corbis; p.129(T): © Henning Delhoff/Science Photo Library; p.129(R): © David Stock/Alamy; p.140/141: © Chelsea Lauren/Getty Images; p.145: Getty Images; p.145(BL): © Yuri Arcurs/Shutterstock; p.146(1): © Alen D/Shutterstock; p.146(2): Takayuki/Shutterstock; p.146(3): Fuse/Getty Images; p.146(4): Goodluz/Shuttterstock; p.146(5): © Yuri Arcurs/Shutterstock; p.158: Quertia/epa/Corbis; p.163(TL): © Benjamin Wiesse/Corbis; p.163(BR): Getty Images; p.165(BL): Sic Stock/Corbis; p.165(BR): Hero/Corbis; p.176/177: Pasieka/Science Photo Library; p.183: © Claus Lunau/Science Photo Library.

Video stills on p.181 from Simons, D. J., & Chabris, C. F. (1999). Gorillas in our midst: Sustained inattentional blindness for dynamic events, Perception, 28,1059-1074. Simons, D. J., & Levin, D. T. (1998). Failure to detect changes to people during a real-world interaction. Psychonomic Bulletin and Review, 5, 644-649.

All other video stills by kind permission of © Discovery Communication, LLC 2014

Corpus

Development of this publication has made use of the Cambridge English Corpus (CEC). The CEC is a multi-billion word computer database of contemporary spoken and written English. It includes British English, American English and other varieties of English. It also includes the Cambridge Learner Corpus, developed in collaboration with Cambridge English Language Assessment.

Dictionary

Cambridge dictionaries are the world's most widely used dictionaries for learners of English. Available at three levels (Cambridge Essential English Dictionary, Cambridge Learner's Dictionary and Cambridge Advanced Learner's Dictionary), they provide easy-to-understand definitions, example sentences, and help in avoiding typical mistakes. The dictionaries are also available online at dictionary.cambridge.org. © Cambridge University Press, reproduced with permission.

Illustrations

Rick Capanni (HL Studios) pp163, 169, 170, 173, 187, 190, 191; Oxford Designers & Illustrators pp24, 28; Simon Tegg pp78, 82, 89

Picture research by Alison Prior

Typeset by emc design ltd